RUSTIC

RUSTIC

Simple food and drink, from morning to night

Photography by Helen Cathcart

FERNANDEZ & WELLS

hardie grant books

Contents

Introduction

First, there was the smell of coffee. Proper coffee. Ten years ago, believe it or not, there were few, if any, places to get such a thing in London. One of these, Monmouth Coffee, in Monmouth Street, Covent Garden, stood out as a beacon of excellence, with an old 1930s Whitmee roaster on site, large hessian sacks of single-estate beans from around the world (sometimes used as alternative seating in the tiny space) and a single-minded dedication to produce flavoursome filter coffee. It was magical, and the cramped wooden seating booths encouraged conversation with strangers – an experience less prevalent today perhaps in the age of the smartphone.

It was at this rather unique coffee shop on Monmouth Street that we first met, some time in 2005. Jorge was manager there; I was working as a journalist for the BBC World Service and based at Bush House on the Strand.

Snatched conversations over time and enthusiasms in common (plus the discovery that our respective wives both had roots in the same Greek island), led to Jorge's mention in passing one day that a certain Nick Lander, food writer and consultant, had asked him if he'd be interested in opening a place on London's newly developed South Bank. Egged on by me, a visit and subsequent pitch for the space was made by the fledgling Fernandez & Wells partnership. The 'business plan' consisted of a cardboard box of what we saw as the core products: a bag of coffee, a slice of plain butter cake, a loaf of crusty sourdough bread, a salami, a hunk of English Cheddar and a bottle of wine. Needless to say we didn't get the South Bank site, but it sowed the seeds and the idea of a few key products, of certain quality and provenance, at the heart of the Fernandez & Wells offer, which has remained our guiding principle.

Much discussion and many more cups of coffee, and we decided the time was right for both of us to head in a new direction and open up our own place. Quite what this was going to be or where took a while to hone, but that it would be a success was never in doubt. The reasoning behind this blind confidence was simple: we would create a place that was stylish but homely with an offer that reflected a taste for timeless quality produce: bread, cheese, cured meats, wine and of course excellent coffee, and a small selection of 'home-baked' cakes. What more could anyone want?

After six months or so of wandering the streets, exploring potential sites and deciding on a name, it became clear, that, for a first site, making an impact was vital. And with its central location, longstanding connection to the world of film and advertising, its still slightly seedy allure and surprisingly reasonable rents, Soho ticked all the boxes.

Once that was decided, attention fairly quickly homed in on the area around Lexington Street and Beak Street, both of which contained some charming but run-down eighteenth-century townhouses with shops beneath. In fact, bang on the corner of the two, one such place was temporary home to a very dubious 'all-you-can-eat for £3' Thai buffet. Standing on the opposite corner, we imagined this becoming our wine bar, and then the little raggedy clothes boutique up for sale a few doors away on Lexington Street

would be the café/deli. Attempts to negotiate a deal with the landlord on the corner proved fruitless, however, and attention focussed on the place on Lexington Street, at number 43, almost opposite Andrew Edmunds' eponymous restaurant and print shop.

Having secured a ten-year lease for what seemed like a reasonable rent, with the help of architect and friend William Tozer, we set about turning the ground floor and basement into a food and wine bar that had the feel of a continental market stall. This entailed stripping it back to the original Georgian wood panelling, painting it white (RAL 9010 with a touch of flat oil), finding some large planks of French oak for the bar and laying York stone paving slabs on the floor.

Keeping it simple was key to reflecting the offerings, which in the first instance were bread, large hunks of cheese, cured meats and wine. The little basement 'kitchen' was used to prepare chunky sandwiches that were piled high on the counter, and since we were in the middle of winter, soups and stews were also added to the menu. By hanging several large legs of jambon noir de bigorre ham from the French Pyrenees in the window before our first day of opening, local curiosity was aroused and ensured a decent showing of customers from the start.

The only downside was that there was no room to do coffee! The gods of Soho smiled on us, however, when two months later a newsagent around the corner at 73 Beak Street came up for sale. A similar Georgian building with a wonderful Soho street view, once stripped back to its original panelling and floorboards, allowed us to complete the Fernandez & Wells offer with some excellent coffee, sandwiches and cake.

Thus began the Fernandez & Wells journey. From these original two little Soho 'shops' have sprung another four siblings, all driven by the same desire to serve simple food of the best possible quality in spaces that are uncluttered and maintain the integrity of the buildings they occupy.

Soho

To mark the occasion of the first Fernandez & Wells opening in Lexington Street in January 2007, I bought Jorge a copy of *Soho Night & Day* by Frank Norman and Jeffrey Bernard. Published in 1966, with its black-and-white photos and first-person journalistic meanderings, it captured the essence of Soho of a particular era, an era that continued to have a certain nostalgic appeal.

In the 1970s, a decade later than the publication of *Soho Night & Day*, my own experience of Soho was informed by a school outing to the British Museum. After a brief survey of ancient Greek pottery, and perhaps stirred by the erotic poses of some of the silhouetted figures, my friends and I bunked off in search of 'a little vice' in Soho, as Frank Norman would have it. As with so many before and since, the experience of pushing through heavy velvet curtains to the grubby inner sanctum of a strip joint to catch a glimpse of forbidden fruit proved both disappointingly dull and expensive.

Jorge's schoolboy reminiscences echo my own, although his earliest Soho memories stem from visits to Berwick Street market with his father.

A few years on and the changes in Soho, while marked, had not been as dramatic

as elsewhere in London. Ironically, this was largely thanks to the sex industry. As long as it remained in many people's eyes an undesirable place to live, the developers were not interested. It was only in the 1980s, with the exposure of police corruption and the closure of dozens of illicit clubs and drinking dens, that the real transformation started.

When we arrived in early 2007 Soho was already quite a different place. While a lot of retail spaces were still fairly shabby, like those we had occupied, new faces of international tech and telecom companies had already set up shop in sleek offices sporting ubiquitous international architecture, adding to the mix of advertising agencies and film production houses that have long been associated with the area. Carnaby Street might have been given an institutionalised facelift, with all the usual high-street suspects, but other corners of Soho managed to resist, nowhere more so than Andrew Edmunds opposite us on Lexington Street. The dark peeling paintwork on the handsome double-fronted Georgian townhouse stands like a bulwark against change, behind which the eponymous restaurant and print shop, the rickety staircase ascending to the writer's watering hole, the Academy Club, and the offices of the Literary Review somehow still hark back to an era that William Hogarth would have recognised.

Many of the traditional trades – the gunsmiths, tailors, lace-makers and printers – have long since disappeared, but a few remain. One such is our near neighbour Bela Pasztor, who has been in his basement metal workshop since 1960, and whose work is still much in demand. And the Cloth House, now in Berwick Street, was an obvious place to source fabric for our first batch of aprons, knocked up by Jorge's mum and Aunt Neli. Memories of Soho's Italian connection linger on, just; with family-run Italian delis like Lina Stores and I Camisa & Son still attracting a loyal clientele.

As for the sex industry, there may still be significant happenings underground but visible remnants, such as the neon-lit alleyway beneath the old Raymond Revuebar sign, are few. Rising rents, changing habits and creeping gentrification have put paid to many of the old clubs and music venues, the legendary Madame Jojo's being just the latest to go.

Perhaps it was the ethos of the small shopkeeper, the artisan trades, so central to Soho that really helped us create in our minds what Fernandez & Wells should be. In the almost ten years that have passed since our arrival, the pace of change has accelerated; cafés, bars and restaurants have proliferated, bringing in a whole new generation of 'hipster' foodies that pack the narrow pavements, alongside Soho's workers and residents, almost every night of the week. It undoubtedly has a great buzz and still retains its diversity and corners of quirky charm, but it's hard not to feel a certain nostalgia for the old Soho, as depicted in the black-and-white photos of *Soho Night & Day*, alongside some apprehension for what lies ahead.

Our Food

Looking back, it is hard to remember which came first – the simple, rustic fare or the shepherd's knapsack. Whatever the case, the latter is often brought to mind when asked about the origins of the food on offer at Fernandez & Wells. Quite where this mythical mountain shepherd came from is not entirely clear; a relative of Jorge's perhaps, living in the foothills of Los Picos mountains in north-western Spain? The point though is that what goes into the knapsack has to be robust, flavoursome and nourishing – a good crusty loaf, a sausage, a hunk of cheese, a slice of butter cake perhaps and a bottle of wine.

Such hearty fare was not always to Jorge's taste. As a young boy he recalls visits to an aunt and uncle in the village of Aleje, in northern León, where, after a long coach journey from Madrid, they would be given a traditional meal of home-made chorizo, farm eggs fried in olive oil and rustic bread, which, along with strong-smelling water pumped from the well, seemed more like a punishment than a treat. But the seeds were sown and from such gustatory memories emerged some of the essence of Fernandez & Wells.

In later years a spell at London's Borough Market developed the instinct for provenance and real quality, which have remained key to selecting Fernandez & Wells products and suppliers. Early friendships there with the likes of Elliott and Alison at the Ham & Cheese Company, Jon Thrupp at Mons Cheesemongers, Neal's Yard Dairy and Monmouth Coffee, have stood the test of time.

That's not to say that the direction Fernandez & Wells has taken was always obvious. A lot of what we do was born out of discovery – apart from coffee, which was a given. The original intention was to set up a café doing espresso really well, accompanied by equally delicious food, in a space that revealed itself. The best example was 73 Beak Street: a former newsagent with fake walls and ceiling, and lino on the floor. All that was required was to strip out the lot, and there, in all their glorious heritage, were the original Georgian wall panelling and wooden floorboards. Using the Fernandez & Wells elements of choice – wood, stone and white paint – with the addition of simple metal stools and blackboards, the transformation into café was simple architectural alchemy.

The same could be said of 43 Lexington Street, although the original offer there was more typical of a classic deli: cheese and meats for sale on the counter, and, bizarrely, a 'tasting glass' of wine, which was all that we were originally permitted to serve under the terms of our license. An unanticipated feature that would prove to be key were the legs of ham hanging in the window. The inspiration for this came from a cycling trip I had made to the Pyrenees, not far from one of the famous Tour de France climbs, the Col du Tourmalet. Lodging nearby in a small hotel, the chef/patron there based his entire menu around the noir de bigorre, a rare-breed black pig native to the region. The foraged diet of nuts and roots give this meat a lovely deep flavour, similar to the Spanish bellota hams. The fact it contains a lot of health-giving oleic acid is an added bonus. Over time, the wine element increased and, apart from the soups and stews at lunchtime, it was the boards of cheese and cured meats that gave it more of a wine-bar feel.

These original two shops, the wine bar at Lexington Street and the café at Beak Street, reflected the split personality of Fernandez & Wells, and it the took a number of years and further sites to bring the two concepts together into what Fernandez & Wells is today: an all-day café bar where you are welcome to come in for food and refreshment from early morning until late at night.

Along the way, whenever things have gone a bit 'off-piste', when ideas are suggested that veer too far from the original path, the spirit of 'Shep' is conjured up and things are swiftly brought back in line. Long may it be so.

Bread

At the start, when we launched Fernandez & Wells, our ideal bread was not that easy to come by. We knew what we wanted: artisan made, preferably organic sourdough with a good crust, which would provide a perfect foil for the sort of cheeses and meats we had in mind for our sandwiches. This might seem straightforward enough nowadays, especially in London, but at the time it proved quite a challenge to source.

One option was the large, round, dark-crusted sourdough loaf made by the French bakery Poilâne, which involved early morning trips to their first London outpost in Chelsea to pick up the few loaves we needed. If you were lucky, your arrival might coincide with a warm croissant or pain au chocolat being taken from the oven, or the occasional bag of 'punitions', delicious small butter cookies. To this day we still use this amazing bread for our toasted cheese sandwich.

As things developed, and despite using a number of different suppliers, we still felt we needed a baker to work with us to develop exactly the sort of style and variety of bread we had in mind. It is hard to remember precisely when we became aware of Syd's presence, but it was some time in 2010 that a shaggy-haired Welshman was seen lurking in the vicinity of the Soho shops. Like a peculiar culinary stalker, he would surreptitiously pop in for a sniff or brief taste of our current sandwich offering. Once contact had been made and his story told, it was obvious that we would go with this baker's bread. Just two of many unique features that made Syd's bread exceptional were the fact his sourdough starter – made from a mix of rye, wholemeal and white organic flours – had been going for an uninterrupted 27 years. The other was that he had hit upon the idea of using buffalo milk whey in his ciabatta mix, simply because a neighbouring stall at the market he frequented had a surplus. This gave them an amazing dark, sweet crust, like no other we had tasted.

Our ideal has always been the most traditional of breads – hard baked so it has a good thick crust with plenty of flavour; a bread you can happily munch away at on its own or with a slab of butter.

With Syd came Dee, an Irish bundle of energy married to a Moroccan chef who seemed to immediately gauge what we were up to at Fernandez & Wells, and who started developing for us her now famous sourdough-based range of cakes. Unfortunately, her parting of the ways with Syd led to us breaking away from him too, but after much soul-searching and tasting we renewed contact with Aleem, a young entrepreneur whose idea of bread again chimed with our own and, just as importantly, who seemed happy to work with us to develop a range exclusively suited to our particular needs. His first tasting tray of viennoiserie was a revelation: the croissant dark and crisp, with a sheen of egg yolk, which harked back to a bygone era.

When we consider sourdough, several things strike us as important: for example, using natural yeasts, not commercial ones, for the starter and using a three-day ferment means the resulting bread is much easier for the body to digest. A lot of digestive problems and allergies stem from the speed with which much modern commercial bread is made today.

Dee would say she has never known any other way. Growing up in Ireland she lived beside a mill that her grandfather had worked in on the Blackwater River near Cork. They always used stone-ground flour to bake loaves on the griddle pan over the fire and there certainly wasn't such a thing as commercial yeast available, so the sourdough effect came by default. Using the same basic principles for her cakes, or what her grandmother would have called 'sweetbreads', Dee now uses a starter of ground almonds, white organic flour and milk, to which you add flour and watch it grow. If it looks like it's dying you add a little sugar to 'feed' it. We feel the taste and texture of these cakes is unique, and fits with our notion of the ideal cake: not too sweet or fancy, but firm and buttery; as fitting to pack for a picnic on a riverbank as with a cup of coffee in Soho.

Cured Meats

The fact we hung legs of ham in the window at Lexington Street before we even opened, meant we had an association with jamon in people's minds from the outset. But it was actually the other cured meats, in particular the saucissons and salamis, that we envisaged being tucked into our notional shepherd's knapsack. One of the first such products we had was the so-called 'there-and-back', by Pierre Oteiza, a champion of the French Basque pig. A long, thin two-piece salami, attached by string, it was given this name simply because such 'saucisse sèche' was traditionally seen as the ideal snack for a journey, one to be eaten on the way there, the other on the way back. This was robust and honest food, fit for the fields, and in many places still being made with the artisanal skills and passion passed on from generation to generation.

But we were no experts, and sourcing the real thing was the key. Again the Borough Market connection proved invaluable, with Brindisa, excellent importer of Spanish goods, and Elliott and his wife Alison at the Ham & Cheese Company. Their tireless efforts and enthusiasm in seeking out some of the best small producers in France and Italy hugely assisted our aim of offering simple quality food that needs no fussing with, that speaks for itself. Choosing wines to complement these products has added to the pleasure.

Clearly though, there was a demand for jamon and it wasn't long before we added a top notch Ibérico in the window alongside the jambon noir de bigorre. The choice was made for us when we were approached by the family firm of Juan Pedro Domecq, whose 36 month cured Ibérico de bellota hams, from lampiño pigs, hit the mark. But finding the right meat is one thing, finding the right people to train to look after and carve them properly is another.

They tend to fall into two categories: those who come with it in their blood and those who combine dexterity with a keen eye for detail. Carving put simply requires really good knife skills to cut perfect slivers from all sections of the leg, in order to achieve the 'melt-in-the-mouth' sensation that jamon is so famed for. Also, given that over 50 per cent of the leg is bone, rind and non-edible fat, it is paramount from a commercial point of view that a leg costing several hundred pounds yields maximum value.

Indeed the value of such prized jamon is not lost on our employees. On one occasion at the end of a long evening at Lexington Street, a young lad who had sauntered in with his friend took it upon himself to grab a whole leg of jamon from the window and make off with it. Whether out of loyalty or foolhardiness, a member of staff gave chase up Beak Street and caught up with him, retrieving the jamon intact and receiving a spontaneous round of applause from the crowd of drinkers on the pavement outside the Sun & 13 Cantons.

After some judicious enquiries the following day it turned out that the lad was, perhaps appropriately, employed as a 'runner' for a nearby media production house and he'd done it for a bet.

Unlike myself, Jorge was brought up in a culture of cured meats, with members of his family curing their own chorizo and suchlike. A particular memory is the smell of his aunt's home-cured cecina in the old stone house in León. While all of our cured meat products are from pig, the cecina de León is the notable exception. This traditional cut of air-dried hind leg of beef, when sliced thinly, has great depth of flavour and is hugely popular on its own or with a plate of fried eggs.

In the Britain of my childhood it seemed that cold cuts of cooked meat were the norm, and cured sausage something of a curiosity, to be found in specialist delicatessens. Attitudes have changed hugely though with travel abroad on the continent and the increased availability of such foods. Also, more and more farms and smallholdings in Britain are experimenting with curing meats, making their own version of salamis and prosciutto. Jorge even had a go himself, having been given a leg of rare-breed pig by Peter Gott from Sillfield Farm, in the early days of Borough Market. Although 'home grown' is a very different product from the continental equivalent, it will be interesting to see how this trend develops in the years to come.

Coffee

1

THE IMPORTANCE OF COFFEE
BY JORGE FERNANDEZ

As a young child I would sit on my Aunt Ana's lap as she dipped sugar cubes into her coffee and allowed me to eat them. This was the era of Nescafé. Milk would be heated in a pan and she would make her version of a modern-day latte. As with most southern European families, coffee was ever-present. Every household owned a stovetop moka pot and the sound of the rising water, its splurts and splutters, remains to this day in my memory – as does the evocative smell.

Fast forward to 1995, and upon returning to London from a year in Madrid, it was a fortuitous meeting with my big sister Ana Maria at the newly opened Seattle Coffee Company in London that set me on my journey into the world of coffee. A sign hung in the shop window saying 'Baristas Wanted'. In need of some cash, and with my sister's encouragement, I offered myself and got the job. Until Seattle Coffee Company's arrival in the UK, the coffee scene had been monopolised by old Italian cafes selling over-heated, frothy cappuccinos.

Vividly, I remember the first coffee tasting I attended, organised by the then roasters for Seattle, Jeremy Torz and Steven Macatonia. They lined up several 'origins' for us to 'cup'; we were instructed to crack the crust with the spoon we had been given, pushing away the grinds to reveal the liquor beneath. My love affair with 'monsoon malabar' coffee ensued.

The energy and buzz that accompanied the coffee scene in the late-1990s was very seductive. What was meant to be a means of earning some holiday cash ended up as the beginnings of a career.

It was another coffee tasting that proved a turning point. Seated in one of the booths at Monmouth Coffee Company with the owner, Anita Le Roy, I was presented with a cup of Ethiopian yirgacheffe. It was a revelation, both in terms of how coffee could or should be roasted; what initially tasted like an exotic tea was transformed into liquid caramel with the addition of milk. I had discovered my teaching master and so, in 1999, I began working for Monmouth Coffee Company, along with friend and partner in crime Gwilym Davies, who was to become a future World Barista Champion. The six years spent at Monmouth were incredibly formative and I enjoyed it all immensely. Anita managed to instil in me her obsessiveness with detail, quality and the importance of provenance, all of which became the founding blocks for Fernandez & Wells.

From the outset, our approach to coffee was simple – a continuation of a more classical style, where neither the introduction of peaches or bananas are desired or required. Rather, we seek inherent sweetness and depth of flavour, resulting in a well-balanced, elegant yet fuller-bodied cup.

Contemporary coffee culture actively seeks brighter, fruitier, more acidic notes with a fashion for roasting coffees, including those used for espresso, ever lighter. We favour a longer, darker roast, which many might consider old-fashioned.

Our coffee roaster, Stephen Leighton, is continuously sampling and buying new coffees, and our espresso blend changes according to the season and the flavour profiles we desire in the cup. There has, in recent years, been a welcome proliferation of independent coffee shops, each bringing their own take on how coffee should be best made. This growth has come hand-in-hand with a multitude of theories and technologies, both new and revived, involving pH levels, temperature, timing and so on. However, it is our view that there's no right or wrong way. Only through the joy of experimentation and development of intuition can the true wonders of coffee be unlocked.

It was in this spirit that the Fernandez & Wells 'Stumpy' came to be. What we were doing already felt quite revolutionary, with the first commercial Synesso coffee machine in the UK, which sat on the counter like a shiny new car, and pulling shots using a massive 33 g (1¼ oz) of Monmouth coffee. Jack Coleman and I enjoyed drinking coffees from a collection of quirky glasses, one of which, being short and stout, came to be known as the Stumpy. This slightly shorter, stronger version of the now-commonplace flat white quickly developed a cult following, so much so we decided to trademark the name. It set the bar for our coffee offer, which remains small with the emphasis on quality rather than quantity.

We appreciate that not everyone is going to have a Synesso machine lurking in their kitchen at home, and it is for this reason we would like to share with you our favourite method of brewing coffee along with some simple steps to make it.

Single Cup Filter

You will need freshly roasted, well-sourced beans; a grinder; a filter cone and filter paper; a kettle; and a cup.

Start with some freshly roasted coffee – by which I mean beans that have been allowed to rest one week from date of roast and preferably no more than three weeks. I have, however, been known to drink coffee well into its sixth week and still enjoy it. There are many kinds of filter cones available on the market; my favourite is a black plastic one by Melitta, for the reason that they don't chip in the sink. For the filter paper we use Filtra in size 2k. There are many grinders available, including some quite good hand-grinders which do the job. You will also need a kettle and the right cup. Each to their own when it comes to cups, but we prefer to use cups, or mugs, that hold up to 200 ml (7 fl oz) of water.

As a rule we use 25 g (1 oz/a good handful) of roasted coffee beans per 200 ml (7 fl oz) of water. Grind the coffee beans while the kettle boils. You'll need to experiment to get the grind right for you, but, as a guide, you want it to look and feel like powder while coarse enough to still feel slightly gritty.

Place the filter cone on top of the cup with the filter paper on top. Flush a little hot water from the kettle through the filter paper. Pour away the water in the cup and replace the filter cone. This process will not only remove any potential flavour taints from the paper but also heat your cup. Next put your ground coffee into the cone and, using water that is just off the boil (leave the kettle for a couple of minutes), pour a little over the top of the coffee to pre-infuse it. You should see a kind of mini volcanic reaction from the coffee, bubbling with a creamy froth, which is an indicator of freshly roasted and ground coffee. If it is not freshly ground or freshly roasted the effect is far less dramatic and flat. The key here is not to allow the grounds to compact, so keep adding water at a steady rate until you remove the cone to expose a cup of wonderful coffee. Simple.

This process should take no longer than three minutes from start to finish. The wonderful thing about making coffee this way is it allows you to taste and compare coffees from any farm, estate or country of origin and really get an appreciation for the subtle characteristics and nuances of the individual beans. By allowing water to flow through without the use of any pressure other than that of gravity we believe the true character of the coffee is drawn into the cup.

Cakes

Banana Loaf with Italian Butter

Makes 1 loaf

4 eggs
170 g (6 oz/¾ firmly packed cup)
    soft brown sugar
80 ml (2½ fl oz) sunflower oil
80 ml (2½ fl oz) buttermilk
170 g (6 oz/1⅓ cups) plain
    (all-purpose) flour, plus 1 teaspoon
    for dusting
1 teaspoon bicarbonate of soda
    (baking soda)
3 very ripe bananas, mashed
1 teaspoon butter for greasing,
    plus extra to serve

We make this cake every day and serve it warm with a loaded knife of the finest Italian butter; just slice and sit it under the grill (broiler) for three minutes. You will need to chill the cake mixture overnight, so allow two days to make this perfect banana loaf.

Whisk the eggs and the sugar together in a bowl until smooth and creamy.

While continuing to whisk, add the sunflower oil to the bowl. Once the oil is combined add the buttermilk and whisk some more.

Sift in the flour and bicarbonate of soda, and use a spatula to fold this into the egg mixture. Once everything is combined, fold in the mashed banana.

Pour the mix into a large plastic container and cover. Place in the fridge and chill overnight. The buttermilk and bicarbonate of soda slowly react to give the cake a good rise and soft texture.

Remove the mixture from the fridge 1 hour before baking. Preheat the oven to 180°C (350°F/Gas 4), and butter and flour a 1.2 litre (2 pint) loaf tin.

Pour the batter into the prepared tin and bake for 1 hour 15 minutes. A skewer inserted into the middle of the loaf will come out clean when the cake is done. Leave the loaf to cool in the tin for about 10 minutes and then serve with butter while still warm, or leave to cool completely on a wire rack.

Cakes

Mini Chocolate Cakes with Prunes

Makes 12 muffin-sized cakes

240 g (8½ oz) unsalted butter,
  plus extra for greasing
250 g (9 oz/2 cups) self-raising flour,
  plus extra for dusting
150 g (5 oz) stoned prunes
200 ml (7 fl oz) water
400 g (14 oz) dark (bittersweet)
  chocolate, broken into pieces
240 g (8½ oz/1 cup) caster
  (superfine) sugar
6 eggs, lightly beaten
25 g (1 oz/¼ cup) cocoa powder,
  plus extra to serve

Preheat the oven to 180°C (350°F/Gas 4) and butter and flour a 12-hole muffin tray. In a small saucepan, cook the prunes in the water over a medium heat for 10 minutes until soft, then mash them with a fork into a purée. Set aside.

Place a large heatproof bowl over a saucepan of gently simmering water, but make sure the bottom of the bowl doesn't touch the water. Melt the chocolate and butter in the bowl, stirring all of the time, until the mixture has completely melted and has a uniform colour and consistency. Remove the bowl from the pan and set on a tea towel on the worktop.

In a separate bowl, lightly beat the sugar and eggs together, then pour this into the chocolate mixture and beat to combine.

In another bowl, sieve the flour and cocoa powder together, then gradually fold this into the chocolate mixture until completely combined. Finally, fold in the prune purée.

Divide the batter evenly among the muffin holes and bake in the oven for 15–20 minutes. The cakes should still be squidgy in the middle. Serve with a dusting of cocoa powder.

Cakes

Coffee and Walnut Loaf

Makes 1 loaf

This loaf is fantastic served with milky coffee. It's also great served with a dollop of maple syrup at breakfast time.

1 teaspoon butter
1 teaspoon plain (all-purpose) flour
250 g (9 oz/2 cups) self-raising flour
½ teaspoon ground nutmeg
250 g (9 oz/scant 1⅓ cups)
   soft brown sugar
250 ml (8½ fl oz) light olive oil
6 eggs
100 ml (3½ fl oz) espresso
100 ml (3½ fl oz) double
   (heavy) cream
200 g (7 oz/1½ cups) chopped
   walnuts

Preheat the oven to 180°C (350°F/Gas 4). Use the butter and plain (all-purpose) flour to butter and flour a 1.2 litre (2 pint) loaf tin.

Mix the self-raising flour, nutmeg and sugar together in a large bowl.

Add in the remaining ingredients and beat with a hand whisk until you have a smooth batter.

Pour the batter into the prepared tin and bake for approximately 55 minutes or until the cake springs back to the touch.

Breakfast

2

STARTING THE DAY

Soho is rightly known for its night-time activities, but arguably the best time to be there is at the crack of dawn. Part of what drew us to the café on Beak Street was the sunrise over Great Pulteney Street viewed from the front window, before Soho awakes and the steam from the coffee machine casts silvery shadows on the old wood panelled walls. There'll be a few early birds about: the cleaners, the delivery vans distributing bread, milk, fruit and veg, and around the corner on Berwick Street the market traders begin to set up their stalls.

To set the tone for the trading day, the shop fronts are swept and washed down, continental-style, while inside the counter display is prepared and the all-important process of 'dialling in' the coffee machine takes place to ensure the first customer through the door at 7.30 am will enjoy a coffee exactly as it should be.

A day in the life of Fernandez & Wells starts a lot earlier for the kitchen, which, like every household, is the heart of the enterprise. There they look forward to the arrival of the barista for their treat of a first coffee of the day. As the local streets come to life, the sandwiches, cakes and other provisions are delivered by car or bicycle depending on the site.

As the first customers arrive, breakfast officially gets underway. Firm believers in the importance of a good breakfast, my favourite Fernandez & Wells combination is Egg Mayonnaise and Black Pudding in a bun (see page 61) with a pot of strong Barry's Irish tea. Jorge prefers a toasted ham, cheese and tomato croissant and a 'Stumpy'. Other options include the Fernandez & Wells Porridge (see page 46), which is made simply with Flahavan's Irish oats and milk (or water for the purists), and garnished with honey and nuts; eggs fried in olive oil with sourdough toast and thinly sliced cecina, the air-dried beef speciality of León (see Khlia-style Fried Eggs on page 55); and the toasted Banana Loaf with Italian Butter (see page 36) has legions of followers.

Porridge

Porridge with Honey and Almonds

Serves 4

Turning oats into porridge is such a simple thing, but everyone seems to have their own take on it. Childhood recollections are often negative when it comes to porridge, viewed as either lumpy grey stodge or watery gruel. Made with care though, and served with a dash of cream and dark brown sugar, it can bring light and comfort to a dark winter's morning. Choosing good-quality organic oats is important. We use Flahavan's Irish oats, which are the flaked variety and quick to make. The addition of a spoonful of Greek honey and some crushed Catalan almonds give it a delicious nutty, savoury twist.

120 g (4 oz/1 cup) porridge oats (oatmeal)
500 ml (17 fl oz) whole (full-fat) milk
100 g (3½ oz) salted almonds, chopped
4 tablespoons orange blossom honey
3 tablespoons double (heavy) cream (optional)

Pour the oats and milk into a saucepan and leave it to sit for 20 minutes.

Cook over a low heat for 5 minutes, stirring constantly.

Divide the porridge into 4 bowls or use 4 small pans like we do. Scatter over the chopped almonds then drizzle a tablespoon of honey on to each serving. For real decadence you can add a couple of teaspoons of double cream on each bowl.

Toast

Toast is a wondrous thing: a good slice of sourdough, grilled until golden and with a hint of charred crust, then spread with unsalted butter. That and a pot of Barry's Gold Blend Irish tea is the true path to happiness. But should you get side-tracked from this purist goal, toast can also provide the perfect foil for a multitude of spreads – both sweet and savoury. Here are some of our favourites.

Egg Mayonnaise with Ortiz Anchovies

Tightly packed anchovy fillets are widely available in glass jars and tins of all shapes and sizes. We use the premium brand Ortiz for particularly good slow-cured ones from Cantabria.

Morcilla with Aioli

Morcilla, the Spanish version of black pudding, works really well on toast. The mini Catalan ones we use are well spiced with onions and a hint of anis and come tied in balls. Remembering to remove the string, fry them gently in olive oil on a low heat, keep them moving for 6–7 minutes to cook through. They tend to break down with cooking as they absorb the olive oil making it easy to mash on to the toast. Serve with aioli and a sprinkling of chopped parsley.

Ortiz Sardines with Unsalted Italian Butter

Every store cupboard should have a tin or two of sardines as an instant snack or meal when the need arises. The Ortiz sardines are fished in Galicia and prepared fresh in the traditional way using virgin olive oil, then packed into tins by hand. Served on hot buttererd toast, they are immensely satisfying. As an extra indulgence we use unsalted Italian butter, Burro Antica Cremeria from Montanari & Gruzza. Just make sure the sardines are topped off with a squeeze of fresh lemon.

Heritage Tomatoes with Garlic and Sea Salt

This is our staple light lunch throughout the summer months. Good quality, ripe Heritage tomatoes are the key, sliced up and mixed with finely chopped garlic, a liberal amount of olive oil and sea salt. Serve with a sprinkling of shopped parsley.

León Chorizo Picante with Heritage Tomatoes

Smoked over oak, this spicy hot version of cooking chorizo from León works really well with the sweetness of the Heritage tomatoes. We slice the sausage lengthways and grill it gently, turning slowly for about 8 minutes. Take care as these have a tendency to spit oil when cooking.

Jams

Strawberry and Thyme Jam

Makes 650 g (1 lb 7 oz)

This isn't really a jam in the traditional sense but more like a type of spread. It can be made as a quick treat to enjoy with freshly made scones or bread and plenty of butter. You can also make it with blackberries or plums when they are season and are plentiful or with pears when you should add a lump of butter and brown them first before adding the other ingredients.

1 kg (2 lb 3 oz) strawberries (British
in-season are best)
250 g (9 oz/1⅓ lightly packed cups)
soft brown sugar
2 sprigs thyme
150 ml (5 fl oz) water

Put all of the ingredients into a large heavy-based saucepan and simmer over a gentle heat for 20 minutes, stirring occasionally. Leave to cool completely.

Remove the woody stems of the thyme and discard. Spoon the jam into clean sterilised jars with a good seal and keep in the fridge for up to 7 days. Note that as this isn't a traditional jam; it won't keep for quite as long.

Eggs

Eggs are the ultimate all-day breakfast food and best done as simply as possible with fresh, well-sourced eggs. At Fernandez & Wells we use free-range farm eggs supplied by Clarence Court, in particular, the special old Cotswold variety known as Mabel Pearman's Burford Browns. They have a dark brown shell and large, deep yellow yolks, and are great for all kinds of cooking. You can find Clarence Court eggs in many supermarkets now, so we definitely recommend you give them a try

Khlia-style Fried Eggs

Serves 1

Khlia is the name used in Morocco for a type of dried meat that is sliced and mixed in with fried eggs. At Fernandez & Wells we use cecina de León – a traditional lean cut of beef that is dry cured and sliced thinly – with a couple of fried eggs and sourdough bread.

Fried Eggs with Za'atar

Serves 1

Two fried eggs served with a drizzle of olive oil and sourdough toast. The sprinkle of za'atar, a traditional Middle Eastern mix of spices, sesame and salt, adds a touch of warmth from the souk.

Fried Eggs with Yoghurt and Harissa Oil

Serves 1

500 ml (17 fl oz) olive oil, plus
 extra for frying
4 tablespoons harissa paste
 (see page 225)
2 eggs
85 g (3 oz) whole (full-fat) milk
Greek yoghurt, to serve
crusty bread, to serve

Make the harissa oil by adding the olive oil to the harissa paste in a glass bottle and giving it a vigorous shake.

Heat a little oil in a frying pan and gently fry the eggs over a medium heat until cooked to your liking. While the eggs are frying, warm a plate in a low-temperature oven. Once the eggs are cooked, transfer them to the warmed plate and add the Greek yoghurt and a good gulp of the harissa oil. Serve with crusty bread.

Egg Mayonnaise
and Black Pudding

We made the mistake of taking this off the menu once at Fernandez & Wells and suffered a storm of protest from a loyal band of regulars as a result. Our customers see this as their brunchtime staple. Since we put it back on, its reputation as a Fernandez & Wells classic has steadily grown.

Everyone has their own favourite type and recipe for black pudding. On the recommendation of old friends living north of Inverness in Scotland, we have always used one by Grants of Speyside; it grills well and has just the right texture to sit on a bed of creamy yellow egg mayonnaise in a sourdough bun.

It has to be said that the black pudding goes equally well with a variety of ways of serving eggs, not least the straightforward 'breakfast-in-a-bun' – simply adding a beautifully cooked fried egg on top, allowing the runny yolk to seep into both the black pudding and bun. If you prefer your black pudding without the bread, scrambled eggs are a good option: gently stir the raw egg in a pan with melted butter over a low heat. Once the correct creamy consistency is achieved remove from the heat, add a little knob of butter to stop it cooking and spruce it up with a sprinkling of chopped chives. Simple.

Omelettes

Chorizo and Manchego

Serves 1

While the delicacy of a plain omelette is often seen as a test for chefs, the addition of Spanish manchego cheese and Alejandro cooking chorizo give this one real presence. Good fresh eggs are essential and the deep yellow yolk from those of the Burford Brown hens we use is amazing.

2 eggs
salt and freshly ground black pepper
1 tablespoon olive oil
125 g (4 oz) chorizo, cut into
  1 cm- (½ in-) thick pieces
50 g (2 oz) manchego

Beat the eggs in a bowl until well combined and season.

Pour the oil into a large frying pan (skillet) over a medium heat and when the oil is hot add the chorizo. Fry it for 3 minutes, stirring occasionally.

Reduce the heat and tip the beaten eggs into the pan. Cook for another 3 minutes, until the egg has set firm underneath but is still slightly runny on top. Fold one side of the omelette into the middle, then fold the other side over. Flip the omelette over and cook for 1 more minute.

Transfer to a plate and shave the manchego over the top of the omelette; the cheese will start to melt.

Tuna and Tomato

Serves 1

Use the best tinned tuna you can find for this omelette, such as Ortiz, whose white bonito tuna is individually line-caught during the season off the Spanish coast.

2 eggs
salt and freshly ground black pepper
1 tablespoon olive oil
75 g (2½ oz) Isle of Wight
  or good-quality tomatoes, sliced
75 g (2½ oz) tinned tuna
buttered sourdough, to serve

Prepare the eggs and heat the pan as on the previous page, then add the tomatoes in place of the chorizo and cook them for 3 minutes. Pour in the eggs and flake the tuna evenly over the top.

Cook for 3 minutes, until the egg is set underneath, then fold and flip the omelette as before. Serve with a slice of buttered sourdough.

Tuscan Ham and Comté

Serves 1

Made from unpasteurised cow's milk in the Franche-Comté region of eastern France, Comté cheese has a similar texture and nuttiness to manchego but with a slightly sweeter taste.

2 eggs
salt and freshly ground black pepper
1 tablespoon olive oil
65 g (2¼ oz) thinly sliced ham
65 g (2¼ oz) Comté, thinly sliced
buttered sourdough, to serve

Prepare the eggs and pan as on the previous page, cook the eggs for 3 minutes until set underneath, then add the ham.

Fold and flip the omelette as before and serve with the Comté and a slice of buttered sourdough.

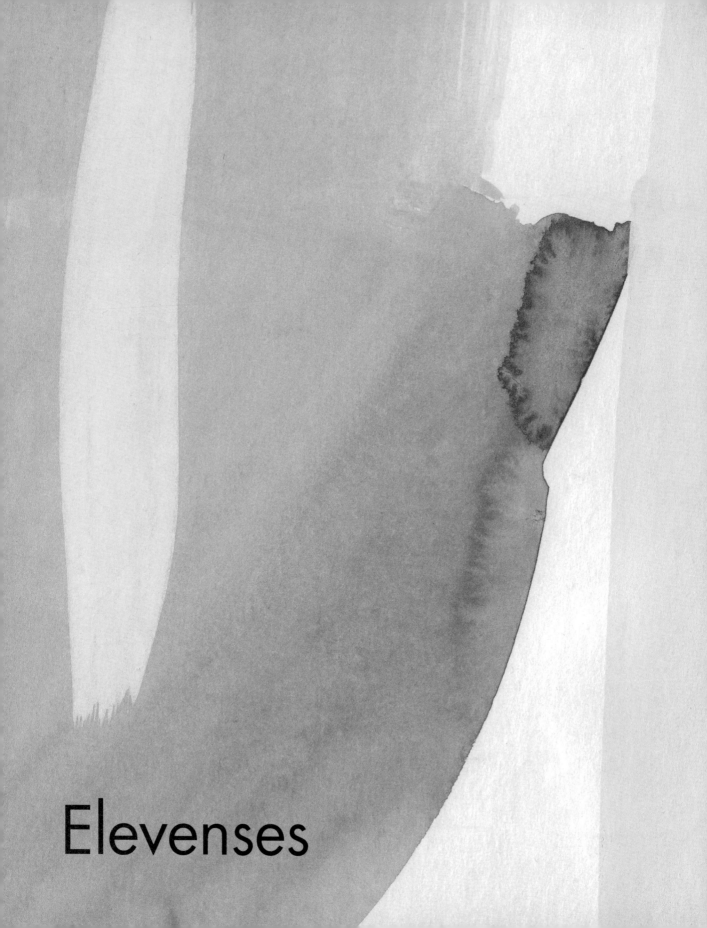

Elevenses

3

THE MID-MORNING SNACK

Elevenses always seems like a peculiarly British thing, but with a little research it appears the phenomenon is widespread across many places and cultures. As with its afternoon equivalent, teatime, habits and expectations vary widely. Depending on what time your day starts, there is often that gap that somehow arises between breakfast and lunch; a gap that needs filling. Clearly for many urban workers coffee is breakfast, but for those who don't have their fix first thing, 'coffee time' means around 11 o'clock. While a perfect flat white or 'Stumpy' on its own may do the trick, the need invariably arises for a little something to accompany it, which can be either sweet or savoury.

For Jorge, that ideal 'little something' comes in the shape of a Pastéis de Nata (see page 71), the classic Portuguese custard tart, in part a consequence of many years living in the vicinity of Lisboa, the Portuguese patisserie in Golborne Road, Notting Hill. When freshly made, with crisp, flaky pastry and a slightly burned caramelised custard top, they can be seriously addictive; not unlike the perfect madeleine in that sense. One is never quite enough.

On the subject of addictions, one of the more curious food and drink pairings is coffee with a cheese straw. Why it works is hard to say, but it does. And if you're feeling like breakfast was inadequate, the full-on toasted cheese made with Montgomery's Cheddar and finely chopped leek and onion on Poilâne bread grilled to a crisp, also hits the elevenses spot.

Pastéis de Nata

Pastéis de nata, the traditional Portuguese custard tarts, have been a feature of the Fernandez & Wells counter from day one. That's not to say that they have been consistently present on our counters. Their addictive qualities, especially when served with a good espresso, became apparent to both of us while living for a time in the vicinity of London's Portuguese communities in both Stockwell and the Golborne Road area of Notting Hill. They do, however, need to be fresh, and the pastry base suitably crispy – ideally with the custard having a slightly burned, caramelised top. Achieving this consistently is difficult, so we set about trying to make our own. First attempts with our ever-obliging baker Aleem were not a great success and it wasn't until we had the idea of doing our take on a mince pie for Christmas that we had a breakthrough. The use of croissant dough for the base and the addition of spiced fruit mincemeat to the custard proved something of a sensation. This has now been adapted for our version of the famous nata. Absolutely perfect with an espresso.

APPLE &
CINNAMON
CRUMBLE 3.25

BANANA
SOURDOUGH
3.25

PEAR &
DAIRY FRE

ORANGE &
ROSEMARY
MADEIRA 3.25

CARROT COCONUT
-PUMPKIN SEED
VEGAN -DAIRY FREE
3.25

.25

Cakes

Madeira Cake

Makes 1 loaf

In our quest for a simple, firm-textured butter cake, the Madeira seemed to hit the spot. A very traditional English sponge, it can be eaten plain or with butter and jam, and works equally well with a coffee in the morning or with tea at teatime.

175 g (6 oz) salted butter, plus
    1 teaspoon for greasing
250 g (9 oz/2 cups) plain
    (all-purpose) flour, plus 1 teaspoon
    for dusting
175 g (6 oz/¾ cup) caster (superfine)
    sugar
3 large eggs
1 teaspoon vanilla extract
2 teaspoons baking powder
50 ml (2 fl oz) buttermilk

Preheat the oven to 180°C (350°F/Gas 4). Use the teaspoon of butter to grease a 1.2 litre (2 pint) loaf tin, then dust it using the teaspoon of flour.

Cream the butter and sugar together in a large bowl for 5 minutes with an electric hand mixer.

While continuing to beat, incorporate the eggs one at a time and then add the vanilla extract.

Sift the flour and baking powder into the egg mix. Combine well.

Fold in the buttermilk until everything is well combined.

Pour the batter into the prepared tin and bake for 1 hour 30 minutes or until a skewer comes out clean when inserted into the middle of the cake. Leave to cool in the tin for around 10 minutes, then transfer to a wire rack to cool completely.

Cakes

Coffee Glacé Loaf

Makes 1 loaf

175 g (6 oz) salted butter, softened,
    plus extra for greasing
250 g (9 oz/2 cups) self-raising flour,
    plus extra for dusting
125 g (4 oz) whole peeled almonds
175 g (6 oz/scant 1 cup) soft brown
    sugar
3 large eggs
1 teaspoon vanilla extract
1 teaspoon baking powder
125 ml (4 fl oz) cold espresso
250 g (9 oz/2 cups) icing
    (confectioners') sugar, sifted

Preheat the oven to 180°C (350°F/Gas 4), and butter and flour a 1.2 litre (2 pint) loaf tin.

Blitz the almonds in a food processor until they are almost a powder. In a large bowl, cream together the butter and brown sugar until light and fluffy and then beat in the eggs one at a time. Stir in the vanilla extract.

Sift together the flour and baking powder in a separate bowl, then fold into the butter mixture, followed by the almonds and 75 ml (2½ fl oz) of the espresso. Pour the mixture into the prepared loaf tin and bake for 1 hour 15 minutes. Transfer the loaf to a wire rack to cool.

To make the glacé icing, combine the icing sugar in a bowl with the remaining espresso and a little warm water to make a runny icing. Drizzle over the top of the cooled loaf.

Cakes

Eccles Cakes

Makes 6 cakes

It was partly thanks to the inspirational St. John restaurant in London that our interest in this most traditional of English cakes was rekindled. Store-bought versions can be very dull, but freshly made with a generous filling of spicy currants and a crispy, sugary top, it is sublime. Add a chunk of Mrs Kirkham's Lancashire cheese and you have a great alternative dessert – made even better with a glass of Oloroso sherry.

1 pack ready rolled puff pastry

For the filling
75 g (2½ oz/⅓ cup) dark muscovado
* sugar*
250 g (9 oz/1⅔ cups) currants
50 g (2 oz/½ cup) sultanas
½ teaspoon mixed spice
½ teaspoon ras el hanout
zest and juice of 1 lemon

For the topping
1 egg, beaten
2 tablespoons caster (superfine)
* sugar*

Preheat the oven to 180°C (350°F/Gas 4) and line a baking tray with baking parchment.

Put all of the filling ingredients into a stand mixer with the paddle attachment. Mix at the slowest speed for 8 minutes until the mixture is sticky.

Straighten the puff pastry out on to a clean work surface and divide it into 6 equal-sized squares. Divide the filling mixture evenly among the pastry pieces, spooning it into the middle of each square.

Use your finger to dab a little warm water from the kettle round the edge of each square. Hold the square of pastry in the palm of your hand and pull a corner into the middle; press it down on to the mixture. Continue to pull and fold the edges and corners of the pastry in until you form a circle. Place the ball of eccles cake on to the work surface and, with the palm of your hand, press down gently to make the cake about 8 cm (3 in) in diameter. Repeat this process for the remaining 5 squares.

Place the Eccles cakes seam-side down on to the lined baking tray. Brush them with the beaten egg and sprinkle over the white sugar. Carefully make 3 x 1 cm (½ in) cuts in the middle of each cake, then bake in the preheated oven for for 22 minutes. They taste best when they are very brown and caramelised.

FERNANDEZ & WELLS 81

Lunch

4

LUNCHTIME ETIQUETTE

Lunchtime signifies a break from work or whatever it is you are doing; a halfway marker in the day. Sandwiches are the Fernandez & Wells staple when it comes to lunch and from 11 am onwards the counters are stacked with the current seasonal range. From the early days our mythical 'shepherd's knapsack' was key to defining the Fernandez & Wells sandwich: a hunk of crusty sourdough bread, cheese and cured meat; robust food with flavour to keep you going throughout the afternoon. The original favourites have remained pretty much the same: simple to construct and relying on the best possible ingredients. English ham, thickly sliced, with Cheddar cheese and piccalilli in a sourdough bun (see page 92) is the classic example, and the grilled Alejandro chorizo, with rocket (arugula) and red (bell) pepper is still popular (see page 93).

That's not to say more subtle combinations are frowned upon; the 30 month-cured prosciutto di Parma with buffalo mozzarella is a match made in heaven. Add a glass of wine to the mix and a late lunch can easily drift into early evening.

Fernandez & Wells first opened one January, in the depth of winter, so the need for some simple hot dishes became quickly apparent. Soups and stews were rustled up in the tiny basement kitchen of Lexington Street, and as word spread among the Soho media crowd, queues quickly formed for the likes of takeaway cassoulet and Rabbit Stew (see page 176). In more recent years, the Fernandez & Wells version of Taktouka, a Moroccan-style dish of roasted pepper and tomato sauce served in a pan with a poached egg on top (see page 165), has become a popular lunchtime hot dish.

With the advent of spring and summer, the menu varies according to seasonal availability of produce, and lighter cheeses and simple salads are added to the offer. Gazpacho, the Spanish cold tomato soup, is hugely popular on hot summer days, although, after much debate, what is served at Fernandez & Wells is actually Salmorejo (see page 161), the richer, creamier equivalent from Cordoba, and has rightly been renamed as such.

The Cult
Sandwich

It was never really our intention to sell sandwiches at Fernandez & Wells. Starting out with a collection of core products on the counter at Lexington Street, including Montgomery's Cheddar, and salamis and buffalo mozzarella, it seemed a logical step to pack them in generous quantities into our sourdough baguettes in the hope that once experienced, albeit in sandwich form, people would come back and buy more, with perhaps a bottle of wine to take home. Much to our surprise and delight, the lunchtime trade boomed and daily sandwich production took off.

Our chief sandwich maker at the time, based in the tiny Lexington Street basement kitchen, was Marcelo, an Argentinian with Italian roots, whose many and varied skills, coupled with his unending affinity for all things Fernandez & Wells, over the years has led to his position today as the company's finance manager.

Inventing new combinations was both a challenge and a pleasure, picking up ideas as we went along. Some were just reminders of timeless favourites, such as the home-cooked ham and Cheddar in a bun encountered in a pub on a fishing trip to the Usk in South Wales. That and a pint of Uley Old Spot ale inspired our version, with the addition of the classic British relish piccalilli; a sandwich that has become a perennial bestseller.

As an aside, we like the idea of offering mustards and relishes to add to sandwiches as you might do at home. We experimented by making our own piccalilli (see the recipe on page 227), but with a local London supplier of jams and relishes of great quality in England Preserves, we are happy to remain purveyors.

Looking back, this style of rustic, market stall sandwich, so prevalent on the continent was, at the time, pioneering. And the fact that they came piled high on the counter, without refrigeration or any sign of plastic packaging, added to the appeal.

Other favourites of ours include the aged French Comté cheese and salami in a crusty flute, chicken with tarragon aioli in a sourdough bun, and the toasted cheese with English Cheddar (see page 92), chopped leek and red onion on slices of French Poilâne bread.

FERNANDEZ & WELLS 91

Sandwich Fillings

Toasted Cheese

Inspired by the queues of hungry customers drawn to the aromas of melted cheese and grilled toast at London's Borough market, toasted cheese has been on offer at Fernandez & Wells since day one. It's important to use a good quality Cheddar, such as Montgomery's, grated and mixed with finely chopped red onion and leek, and generously heaped between two slices of good sourdough bread. We use Poilâne, the amazing French sourdough loaf with a dark crust, which turns golden brown and crisp as the cheese melts and oozes through. Simple and delicious at any time of day.

Filled Croissant

A legacy of the French re-invention of the croissant as 'fast food' in the 1970s, the filled croissant fills that breakfast gap. The key, as ever, lies in using the best possible products. We use a really good French Comté cheese, which has a sweet nutty flavour that can be combined with slices of ripe Heritage tomato and/or thin slices of free-range English cooked ham. A well-made butter croissant is an essential that also lends itself to gentle grilling until the cheese starts to melt.

Ham, Cheese and Piccalilli

Like a ploughman's lunch in a sandwich, we use Westcombe Cheddar from Neal's Yard Dairy and free-range English ham with good crusty sourdough bread. We have at times made our own Piccalilli, but the one from local jam and pickle specialists, England Preserves, is so good we stick with that.

The Combo

This was inspired by a visit Rick made to the food market in Florence, where sandwiches can be made up by pointing at whatever you fancy. The original 'combination' consisted of thinly sliced Mortadella with a generous dollop of aioli spread on top, followed by slices of salami, fresh rocket (arugula), shavings of Parmesan cheese and finally a generous quantity of wafer thin slices of Parma Ham.

Grilled Chorizo with Rocket and Red Peppers

Served in a crispy sourdough ciabatta, red (bell) pepper and chorizo on a bed of green rocket (arugula) always looks tempting and deserves a special place on the counter. The Alejandro cooking chorizo we use is cut in half lengthways and grilled for a couple of minutes on either side. Although cured, it needs to be well heated through to really bring out the juiciness and flavour and the added pungency of paprika and garlic quickly fills any room.

Classic Tuna with Red Onion, Capers, Olives and Anchovies

Taking care to choose good quality, line-caught tuna, the light freshness of this combination still packs real flavour. All the ingredients are chopped up together, and with the addition of olive oil and fresh lemon juice, mixed into a spreadable paste. A great light lunch with a glass of chilled rosé.

Poached Chicken with Pancetta, Rocket, Tomato and Mozzarella

Chicken is hugely versatile for sandwiches and over the years we have tried a number of combinations. This one using the breast of free-range chicken from Suffolk – poached in a little white wine and a bay leaf helps keep it moist. The organic pancetta we use from Brindisa, sliced thinly and grilled in a little olive oil, adds a touch of smoky saltiness. It's then rounded off with the addition of the fresh tomato and slices of good quality mozzarella.

Salads

Mozzarella, Peaches and Prosciutto

Serves 6

400 g (14 oz) peaches
200 g (7 oz) prosciutto di Parma
4 × 125 g (4 oz) balls of buffalo
    mozzarella
50 ml (2 fl oz) light olive oil
25 ml (1 fl oz) balsamic vinegar
½ teaspoon salt and freshly ground
    black pepper

We use unpasteurised mozzarella di bufala from The Ham & Cheese Co. (see the Favourite London Addresses on page 230) for this recipe, as we love its creamy texture and slightly sour tang, but you can use a pasteurised buffalo mozzarella if you prefer.

Cut the peaches in half and remove the stones. Lay the peach halves in an ovenproof dish and bake for 10 minutes or until they are slightly soft. Remove from the oven and allow to cool.

Thinly slice the prosciutto di Parma if you have not bought it pre-sliced. Drain the mozzarella and tear it into bite-sized pieces.

To assemble the dish, scatter the peaches on to a large, rimmed serving plate and drizzle them with the olive oil and vinegar. Top with the torn mozzarella, then fold over the prosciutto slices and position them around the rim of the of the dish. Sprinkle with salt and pepper, and serve.

Salads

Grilled Asparagus with Parma Ham

Serves 2

small bunch asparagus (British in-season asparagus is best)
1 tablespoon olive oil
2 tablespoons balsamic vinegar
4 thin slices prosciutto di Parma
pinch of sea salt

Heat a griddle pan (ribbed skillet) over a high heat. In a small bowl, toss the asparagus in the oil and lay the spears on to the pan. Fry for 6 minutes, giving the pan a shake from time to time to cook the asparagus evenly. Add in the balsamic and cook for a further 3 minutes.

Transfer the asparagus from the pan to a plate and sprinkle with the salt. Serve with the prosciutto and a couple of sliced and salted heritage tomatoes if you like.

Salads

Chickpea, Chilli and Mint

Serves 4

This salad is delicious without it, but to add another dimension to its flavours you can add some sliced feta; we use unpasteurised barrel-aged feta for even more depth.

For the salad
100 ml (3½ fl oz) olive oil
2 red onions, finely sliced
3 tablespoons harissa paste
  (see page 225)
3 × 400 g (14 oz) tins chickpeas,
  drained and rinsed
4 garlic cloves, crushed
juice of 1 lemon
2 red chillies, deseeded and chopped,
  to serve
300 g (10½ oz) feta, very thinly
  sliced, to serve (optional)

For the dressing
200 g (7 fl oz) whole (full-fat) milk
1 tablespoon Greek yoghurt, more
  if desired
1 tablespoon chopped mint leaves
¼ teaspoon freshly ground black
  pepper
1 tablespoon chopped coriander
  (cilantro) leaves

Combine all of the salad ingredients except the chillies and feta in a large bowl until they are well mixed.

In a separate bowl, whisk together all of the dressing ingredients until thoroughly combined.

Pour the chickpea salad on to a large, rimmed serving plate and dot all over with the dressing. Finally, scatter over the chilli and feta, if using, and serve straight away.

Salads

Courgettes with Lemon and Sea Salt

Serves 4

All of our main dishes at Fernandez & Wells can be served with these delicious grilled courgettes or, of course, you can eat them on their own with plenty of crusty bread.

*3 medium-sized courgettes
(zucchini)
100 ml (3½ fl oz) olive oil
½ lemon
1 teaspoon sea salt*

Cut the courgettes lengthways into 5 pieces and put them into a large bowl along with half of the olive oil. Toss the courgettes in the oil to coat them well all over.

Heat a griddle pan (ribbed skillet) on a high heat. Once the pan is really hot, lay the slices of courgette in a single layer in the pan (you may need to do this in batches) – they should sizzle as soon as they touch the pan if it is hot enough. Griddle for 1 minute then turn over the slices and cook for a further minute, or until charred on both sides.

Transfer the chargrilled courgettes to a clean bowl and pour over the remaining olive oil. Squeeze over the juice from the lemon and sprinkle with salt. Mix well and serve.

Salads

Tomatoes, Sea Salt and Olive Oil

Serves 6

Tomatoes in Britain are invariably a disappointment. Not surprising, perhaps, given the climate, but there's really no excuse for the kind of tasteless, uniformly round version that scarcely dents if you drop it.

It was back in Jorge's Borough Market days, before the advent of Fernandez & Wells, that a stall appeared selling cucumbers and tomatoes from the Isle of Wight. Though he was sceptical at first, these tomatoes were an absolute revelation, akin to the ripe sweet versions we were both used to gorging on during summer breaks in Greece and France. The heirloom (also known as heritage) varieties come in an amazing array of colours, shapes and sizes, and when in season are worth seeking out to make this simple, but stunning salad.

500 g (1 lb 2 oz) mixture of heritage tomatoes
300 ml (10 fl oz) extra-virgin olive oil
100 ml (3½ fl oz) balsamic vinegar
½ teaspoon sea salt
sourdough bread, to serve

Slice each tomato into 6 pieces and put them into a colander over a bowl to allow the excess water to drain from them for 10 minutes.

Whisk the olive oil, balsamic vinegar and salt together in a separate bowl.

Place the drained tomatoes on to a serving plate and pour over the olive oil and balsamic dressing. Serve with buttered crusty sourdough bread to mop up the juices.

Teatime

5

THE BRITISH STAPLE

Few things are more typically British than afternoon tea. As with elevenses, it can be either a sweet or savoury affair (or mix of the two) that serves to fill the gap between lunch and supper. Tea, of course, is the preferred drink, usually served with milk or a slice of lemon. The familiar line up would be sandwiches, cakes and biscuits, a freshly made scone with jam and perhaps some hot buttered toast.

At Fernandez & Wells, cake has come to be an important part of the teatime scene. Not the fancy, overly sweet sort with heaps of icing, which is all style and not a lot of substance. With a nod to the shepherd and his knapsack, ours is the sort of cake you could wrap in a napkin and put in your bag. However, sourcing it was difficult unless it was literally home made and, in the very early days, my wife Cindy filled the gap with her excellent lemon polenta cake. A number of suppliers were tried with mixed success. Then, thanks to our baker at the time, an Irish woman called Dee appeared on the scene and amazingly understood what we were on about. Dee took it upon herself to give our cakes her unique take with the introduction of sourdough into the mix (which is normally associated with bread). This can be a time consuming and difficult process, so in this book we have adapted and simplified the recipes for home baking. Today the olive oil cakes (see pages 135–37) and the Moroccan Honey Cake (see page 120) have become Fernandez & Wells staples.

While the ubiquitous 'all-day' breakfast seems like a contradiction in terms, there is no problem with shifting the emphasis slightly towards 'high tea' in late afternoon, and ordering a plate of fried eggs, possibly with the addition of some choice ham. In the same vein, Ortiz sardines on toast with plenty of unsalted Italian butter makes a satisfyingly healthy snack, which also works well with a cup of black tea.

Cakes

Marrakechi Orange Cake

Makes 1 cake

For the cake
500 g (1 lb 2 oz) unsalted butter, plus extra for greasing
500 g (1 lb 2 oz/2⅔ lightly packed cups) light soft brown sugar
9 eggs
500 g (1 lb 2 oz/4 cups) self-raising flour
1 level teaspoon baking powder
125 g (4 oz/1¼ cups) ground almonds (almond meal)
125 ml (4 fl oz) whole (full-fat) milk
zest of 2 oranges
bunch of mint, finely chopped

For the topping
500 g (1 lb 2 oz/4 cups) icing (confectioners') sugar, sifted
250 g (9 oz) unsalted butter, at room temperature
2 drops of rose water
handful of Lebanese dried rose petals, to decorate (optional)

Preheat the oven to 190°C (375°F/Gas 5), and grease and line a 28 cm (11 in) round springform cake tin.

For the cake, cream the butter and sugar together in a large mixing bowl until light and fluffy. Beat in the eggs one by one until well combined.

Sift the flour and baking powder into a separate bowl and stir in the ground almonds. Fold the flour mixture into the butter mixture in 3 batches.

Gently fold in the milk, orange zest and mint until everything is well combined.

Pour the batter into the prepared tin and bake for 45–60 minutes. A skewer inserted into the middle of the cake will come out clean when it's done. Remove from the tin and allow to cool on a wire rack.

While the cake is cooling, make the topping. Sift the icing sugar into a mixing bowl and add the softened butter. Cream together on a medium speed in a food processor or using an electric hand mixer until the mixture is light and fluffy. Add the rose water and beat for another 30 seconds.

Spread the topping over the cooled cake and sprinkle with the dried rose petals, if using.

Cakes

Sourdough Bread and Muscovado Pudding

Serves 6

1 x 7-day-old sourdough loaf
250 g (9 oz) salted butter
250 g (9 oz/scant 1⅓ cups)
   dark muscovado sugar
20 g (¾ oz) chopped dates
½ teaspoon ras el hanout

For the custard
6 eggs
6 egg yolks
200 g (7 oz/generous ¾ cup) caster
   (superfine) sugar
750 ml (24 fl oz) double
   (heavy) cream
200 ml (7 fl oz) whole (full-fat) milk
1 vanilla pod, split

We very much like the sweet-and-sour nature of this recipe, created by using a seven-day-old sourdough loaf. It is best not to remove the dark outer crusts, which add to the richness of the flavour. This is unlike any other bread pudding you will have made.

Preheat the oven to 180°C (350°F/Gas 4). Slice the bread thinly – leave the crusts on – and butter each slice generously. Cut the buttered slices in half diagonally.

Cover the bottom of an ovenproof dish with a layer of the buttered bread triangles. Sprinkle over some of the sugar and chopped dates, then add another layer of bread and sprinkle that with more sugar and chopped dates. Repeat until you have used up all the ingredients. After you have done your first layer, try to work out how many layers of bread you will ultimately have in your dish and then roughly divide the sugar and dates between them so you will have a fairly even mix throughout the pudding.

To make the custard, whisk together the eggs, egg yolks and sugar in a large heatproof bowl.

Gently heat the milk and cream in a saucepan over a low heat until it is just simmering. Take it off the heat and slowly pour it into the egg and sugar mixture, whisking all of the time. Scrape the seeds into the custard from the split vanilla pod and whisk again to combine. (You can put the pod into a jar of sugar to make vanilla sugar if you like.)

Pour the custard over the bread layers – you may have to do this in stages while you wait for the custard to soak down the layers – and sprinkle with the ras el hanout.

Bake for 40 minutes until the surface is golden brown and the custard is gently bubbling. Serve warm with cream, or leave to go cold, then cut into thin slices and serve with a shot of espresso.

Cakes

Pomegranate and Raspberry Cake

Makes 1 cake

We sell both pomegranate and blood orange juice when it is in season, and that's the inspiration for this cake. We use England Preserves raspberry jam for the glaze and the finished result is one of the most impressive looking cakes we sell.

3 large pomegranates
3 large oranges
1 teaspoon butter, for greasing
1 teaspoon plain (all-purpose) flour, for dusting
9 eggs
450 g (1 lb/4½ cups) ground almonds (almond meal)
450 g (1 lb/2 cups) caster (superfine) sugar
1½ tablespoons baking powder
150 g (5 oz) seedless raspberry jam

Cut the pomegranates in half and, over a bowl with the flesh side down, knock the back of the fruit. The seeds will drop into the bowl. Carefully pick through the seeds to make sure none of the pith is present (discard any bits that have fallen in) and set aside.

Put the whole oranges into a large heavy-based saucepan of water. Bring to the boil over a high heat, then reduce the heat and simmer for 2½ hours.

In the meantime, butter and flour a 28 cm (11 in) round springform cake tin and preheat the oven to 180°C (350°F/Gas 4).

Carefully remove the oranges from the pan to a plate using a slotted spoon and allow them to cool. Cut the cooled oranges in half, remove any seeds, then place them in a food processor. Blitz until you have a smooth paste.

Lightly beat the eggs in a large mixing bowl, then add the almonds, sugar, baking powder and orange paste, and half of the pomegranate seeds.

Pour the mixture into the prepared tin and bake for approximately 1 hour or until golden in colour and the cake springs back to the touch.

Transfer the cake to a wire rack and cool for 30 minutes. Spread the raspberry jam over the top of the cake, then allow cool for another 15 minutes. Sprinkle with the remaining pomegranate seeds and serve.

Cakes

Moroccan Honey Cake

Makes 1 cake that serves 10

This cake is inspired by Dee's family connections with Morocco. Almost two decades ago, returning from a honey-hunting trip north of Rabat with her mother-in-law, they stopped at the side of the road under the shade of a tree. There her mother-in-law lit a small burner, placed a terracotta dish on top and proceeded to make something like a caramel out of melted sugar, honey and almonds. She then made a large, frothy pancake batter, known as a *baghrir*, and poured it on to the browned almonds. Flipped over, the resulting sweet, crispy pancake, sprinkled with orange-flavoured water, was a delight. This cake goes particularly well with fresh mint tea.

500 g (1 lb 2 oz) salted butter, plus extra for greasing
500 g (1 lb 2 oz/scant 2¼ cups) caster (superfine) sugar
8 eggs
400 g (14 oz/3¼ cups) self-raising flour
2 teaspoons baking powder
100 g (3½ oz/1 cup) ground almonds (almond meal)
pinch of salt
100 ml (3½ fl oz) buttermilk
300 g (10½ oz) honey
250 g (9 oz/2 cups) toasted flaked (slivered) almonds

Preheat the oven to 180°C (350°F/Gas 4) and grease a 28 cm (11 in) round springform cake tin.

Cream together the butter and the sugar in a large mixing bowl until light and creamy. Beat in the eggs, one at a time, until well combined.

In a separate mixing bowl, mix together the flour, baking powder, ground almonds and salt.

Fold the dry ingredients into the butter mixture, then pour in the buttermilk and gently mix this in.

Pour the batter into the greased tin, smooth and bake for 45 minutes until the cake springs back when pressed. Remove from the oven and, with the cake still in the tin, slowly drizzle over the honey, allowing it to soak into the cake, and then sprinkle over the flaked almonds. Leave to cool in the tin before slicing and serving.

Cakes

Lemon Teabread

Makes 1 loaf

250 g (9 oz) salted butter, plus extra
    for greasing
250 g (9 oz/generous 1 cup) caster
    (superfine) sugar
4 medium eggs
200 g (7 oz/1⅔ cups) self-raising
    flour
½ teaspoon baking powder
50 g (2 oz/⅓ cup) ground almonds
    (almond meal)
100 ml (3½ fl oz) buttermilk
juice and zest of 3 lemons

For the icing
250 g (9 oz/2 cups) icing
    (confectioners') sugar
juice and zest of 2 lemons
hot water

This came about thanks to Jorge's television habits. Having watched a show with chef Raymond Blanc making a simple but delicious-looking teacake, he reported back to Dee, who in turn came forward a couple of days later with what is now known as the Fernandez & Wells lemon teabread.

Preheat the oven to 180°C (350°F/Gas 4) and grease a 1.2 litre (2 pint) loaf tin.

To make the cake, beat together the butter and the sugar in a large mixing bowl until you have a creamy consistency. Beat in the eggs one at a time, until they are well combined.

Sift in the flour and baking powder, add the ground almonds, then fold into the butter mixture. Fold in the buttermilk. Add the zest and juice of the lemons and make sure they are well mixed in the batter.

Pour the batter into the greased tin and bake for 40 minutes or until the cake springs back when pressed. Leave for 10 minutes then remove from the tin and leave to cool on a wire rack.

When the loaf is nearly cool, make a glacé icing. Sift the icing sugar into a bowl and add the lemon juice. Using a wooden spoon, gradually stir in enough hot water to make a thick paste. Beat until white and smooth, and thick enough to coat the back of a spoon. Pour the icing over the fully cooled loaf. Decorate with a sprinkling of lemon zest, before serving.

Cakes

Orange and Lavender Loaf

Makes 1 loaf

250 g (9 oz) salted butter, plus extra
    for greasing and serving
juice and zest of 2 oranges
1 teaspoon dried lavender
25 g (1 oz) caster (superfine) sugar
4 eggs
200 g (7 oz/1⅔ cups) self-raising
    flour
50 g (2 oz/½ cup) ground almonds
    (almond meal)
100 ml (3½ fl oz) buttermilk

Herbs, when used judiciously in our cakes, can add another dimension to the experience, as in this one.

Preheat the oven to 180°C (350°F/Gas 4) and grease a 1.2 litre (2 pint) loaf tin.

Squeeze the orange juice into a small bowl and stir in the zest and dried lavender. Leave the lavender to soak in the juice for 1 hour.

In a large mixing bowl, cream the butter and the sugar together until you have a light, fluffy consistency. Add the eggs one at a time while continuing to beat.

Fold in the flour and almonds, and then the buttermilk. Finally, add the orange juice with the lavender and zest, and mix to combine.

Pour the batter into the loaf tin and bake for 40 minutes or until the cake springs back when pressed. Allow to cool for 5 minutes and then transfer the cake to a wire rack to cool completely. Serve with some soft, salted butter.

Cakes

Ras el Hanout Loaf with Buttermilk

Makes 1 loaf

1 teaspoon butter, for greasing
250 g (9 oz/2 cups) plain
(all-purpose) flour, plus 1 teaspoon
for dusting
1 teaspoon bicarbonate of soda
(baking soda)
1½ teaspoons ras el hanout
¼ teaspoon sea salt
250 g (9 oz/1⅓ lightly packed cups)
dark muscovado sugar
2 eggs
180 g (6 oz/½ cup) black treacle
(molasses)
250 ml (8½ fl oz) buttermilk
1 tablespoon of icing (see recipe and
method on page 124), to serve
1 long red chilli, deseeded and thinly
sliced, to serve
icing (confectioners') sugar, to serve

In Morocco, ras el hanout is a spice mix generally used in savoury food, but it also works well in sweet recipes. You can buy ras el hanout pre-mixed, but it's easy enough to make your own: mix together a teaspoon of ground cumin and half a teaspoon each of chilli powder, ground cinnamon and ground ginger. Make sure everything is mixed well and store in an airtight jar.

We like to use sel de Guérande for this cake, a sea salt from the salt marshes in southern Brittany, because it is quite delicate and helps get that balance of sweet and savoury this cake requires. The use of buttermilk also keeps the cake moist and it should be kept in an airtight tin for at least two days before you eat it, to allow it to become even more moist and flavoursome.

Preheat the oven to 180°C (350°F/Gas 4) and butter and flour a 1.2 litre (2 pint) loaf tin.

Sift the flour, bicarbonate of soda, ras el hanout and salt into a large mixing bowl and stir in the muscovado.

In a separate bowl beat together the eggs, treacle and buttermilk. Pour this mixture into the bowl containing the dry ingredients and whisk vigorously until well combined.

Pour the batter into the prepared tin and bake for 45 minutes until just cooked – that is until the centre springs back to the touch. Transfer the cake to a wire rack to cool, then store in an airtight container for at least 2 days before serving.

Once ready to serve, drizzle over the icing , top with the sliced chilli and dust with icing sugar.

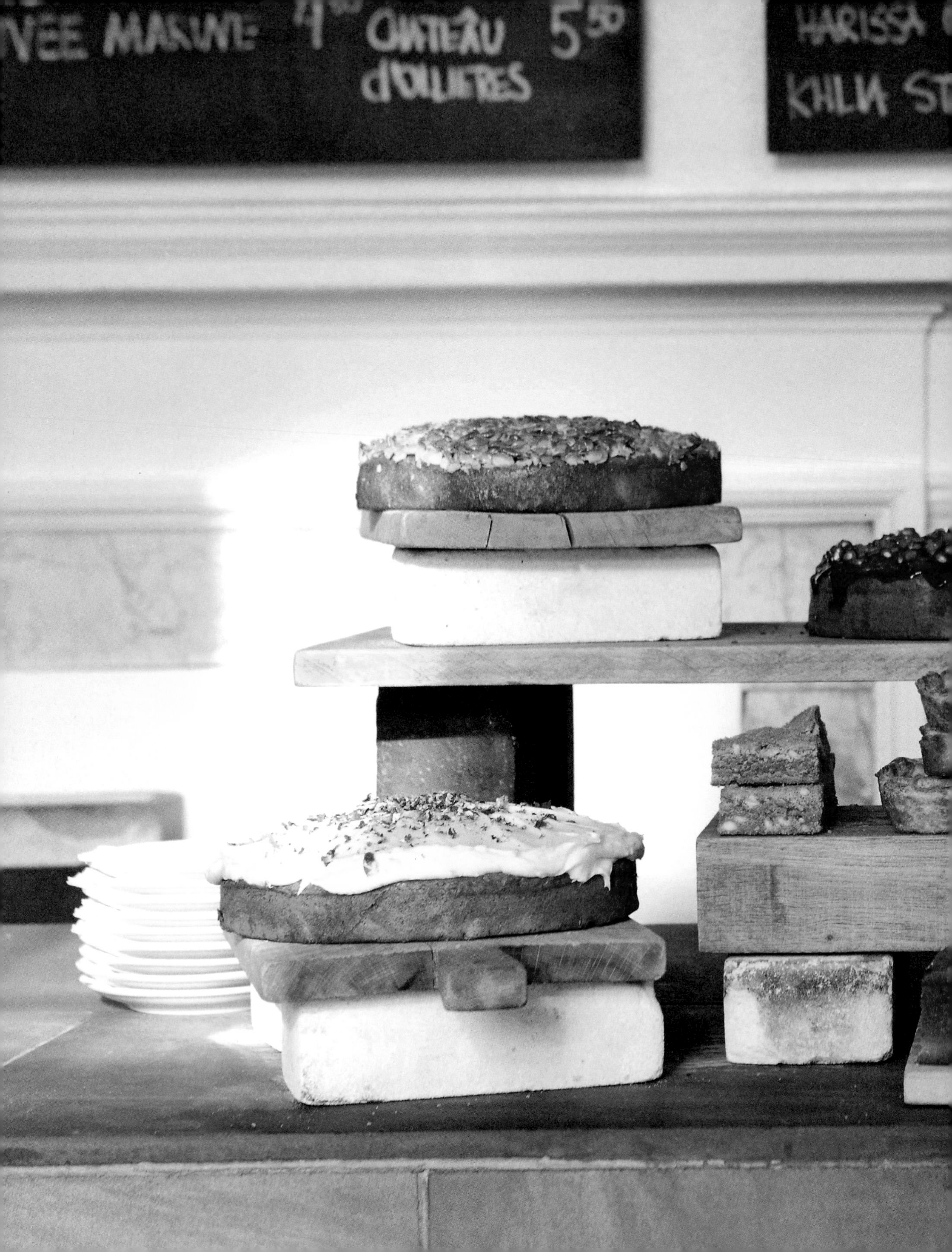
HARISSA

Cakes

Best Madeleines Ever!

Makes 24 madeleines

For years we had asked Dee to produce some madeleines, which she did on occasion when the nagging became too much to bear. Freshly made and placed on the counter at Beak Street, they would disappear in a flash. And that's the problem: they are impossible to resist when warm from the oven. Maybe they are best kept as an occasional treat and made in the relative calm of your own kitchen. You will need two non-stick madeleine trays and the cake mix needs to stand for three hours before transferring to the oven, so allow yourself plenty of time when making them.

2 large eggs
95 g (3½ oz) caster (superfine) sugar
1 teaspoon vanilla extract
½ teaspoon sea salt
110 g (3¾ oz/scant 1 cup) plain
   (all-purpose) flour
1 level teaspoon baking powder
90 g (3¼ oz) melted butter
icing (confectioners') sugar, to dust

Use a hand-held blender to whisk the eggs, sugar, vanilla extract and salt together in a large mixing bowl for about 10 minutes until the mixture is very light in colour and has doubled in size.

Sift the flour and baking powder into the egg mixture, and gently fold to combine. Carefully pour in the melted butter and fold it into the mix. Cover the bowl with a tea towel and set aside for 3 hours.

Preheat the oven to 220°C (430°F/Gas 7). Heat two 12-hole madeleine trays in the oven for 5 minutes. Remove the trays from the oven and immediately fill them three quarters full with the madeleine batter. Bake for 5 minutes, then reduce the temperature of the oven to 190°C (375°F/Gas 5) and bake for another 5 minutes until the cakes are domed and golden in colour. Remove from the tins and leave to cool on a wire rack. Dust with icing sugar, to serve.

Cakes

Olive Oil Cake with Lemon and Rosemary

Makes 1 cake

This has been a hit since the moment we first put it out on the counter at Fernandez & Wells. A gorgeous yellow colour with a baked golden-brown crust, there's something about the olive oil and almonds that makes it feel both health giving and satisfying – not too sweet and beautifully moist, so it lasts well. We do several versions that are all equally delicious.

1 teaspoon butter, for greasing
50 g (2 oz/scant ½ cup) plain (all-purpose) flour, plus 1 teaspoon for dusting
2½ teaspoons baking powder
125 g (4 oz/1¼ cups) ground almonds (almond meal)
200 g (7 oz/generous ¾ cup) caster (superfine) sugar
250 ml (8½ fl oz) light olive oil
5 eggs, lightly beaten
1½ tablespoons chopped rosemary leaves
zest of 2 lemons
fresh raspberries, to serve (optional)

Preheat the oven to 160°C (320°F/Gas 3). Butter and flour a 20 cm (8 in) round springform cake tin.

Sift the flour, baking powder and almonds into a large mixing bowl, tip in the sugar, and stir everything together.

Add the olive oil, eggs, rosemary and lemon zest to the mix and fold together until you have a smooth batter.

Pour the batter into the prepared baking tin and bake for 45–50 minutes; the cake will have a slight wobble when you remove it from the oven, but will set beautifully firm once it has cooled. If the top of the cake seems to be browning too quickly, lay a double-folded piece of baking parchment across the top of the tin. After removing from the oven, leave the cake to cool in its tin until firm enough to transfer to a wire rack. Slice and serve with some fresh raspberries.

Cakes

Olive Oil Cake with Chocolate

Makes 1 cake

1 teaspoon olive oil, for greasing
50 g (2 oz/scant ½ cup) cocoa powder
125 ml (4 fl oz) boiling water
2 teaspoons vanilla extract
170 g (6 oz/1⅔ cups) ground
   almonds (almond meal)
½ teaspoon bicarbonate of soda
   (baking soda)
pinch of salt
225 g (8 oz/1 cup) caster (superfine)
   sugar
170 ml (6 fl oz) light olive oil
3 large eggs
Greek yoghurt or a shot of espresso,
   to serve (optional)

Preheat the oven to 180°C (350°F/Gas 4), and oil and line a 23 cm (9 in) round springform cake tin with baking parchment.

Whisk the cocoa powder into the boiling water in a bowl until you have a smooth paste, then whisk in the vanilla extract.

In a separate bowl, mix the ground almonds with the bicarbonate of soda and salt.

Place the sugar, olive oil and eggs into the bowl of a food processor and beat with the flat beater until the mixture is light in colour and has a creamy texture.

Turn the speed of the processor to low and add the almond mixture and then the cocoa paste. Beat slowly until everything is well combined.

Pour the batter into the tin and bake for 45 minutes or until a skewer inserted into the centre of the cake comes out clean. Transfer to a wire rack to cool, then serve with Greek yoghurt or a shot of excellent espresso.

Cakes

Olive Oil Cake with Apple Compote

Makes 1 cake

1 teaspoon olive oil, for greasing
50 g (2 oz) spelt flour
125 g (4 oz/1¼ cups) ground
   almonds (almond meal)
200 g (7 oz/scant 1 cup) soft light
   brown sugar
2½ teaspoons baking powder
5 eggs, lightly beaten
250 ml (8½ fl oz) light olive oil
2 teaspoons vanilla extract
Greek yoghurt, to serve

For the apple compote
3 large seasonal eating apples,
   peeled, quartered and deseeded
4 tablespoons water
3 tablespoons soft light brown sugar
½ teaspoon sea salt

Preheat the oven to 180°C (350°F/Gas 4), and oil and line a 20 cm (8 in) round springform cake tin with baking parchment.

Begin by making the apple compote. Place the apples in a large heavy-based saucepan over a medium heat and add the water, sugar and salt. Bring to a simmer, then reduce the heat, cover and cook for 15 minutes. Watch that the pan does not dry out; add a drop of water when needed, but not too much otherwise the apples will become mushy. Remove from the heat and set aside.

For the cake, mix the flour, ground almonds, sugar and baking powder together in a large mixing bowl. Add the eggs, olive oil and vanilla extract, and fold into the flour mixture until you have a smooth batter.

Pour the batter into the prepared tin and bake for 45–50 minutes or until a skewer inserted into the centre of the cake comes out clean. Cool on a rack and serve with a spoonful of the apple compote and a spoonful of Greek yoghurt.

Biscuits

Scottish All-butter Shortbread

Makes 12 biscuits

175 g (6 oz) salted butter, plus extra
    for greasing, at room temperature
100 g (3½ oz/scant ½ cup) caster
    (superfine) sugar, plus extra
    to finish
175 g (6 oz/scant 1½ cups) plain
    (all-purpose) flour

This is a classic biscuit with lots of options when it comes to toppings, such as our Benedict Bar, which has the addition of almonds and honey. The plain one with the brown butter crust is great though, and even better with a cup of tea.

Preheat the oven to 180°C (350°F/Gas 4) and butter a 25 × 20 cm (10 × 8 in) baking tray, then line it with baking parchment.

Cream together the butter and sugar in a large mixing bowl for about 5 minutes until smooth.

Add the flour in stages, incorporating it each time. You will need to use your hands to bring everything together as you add more flour as the mixture will start to resemble breadcrumbs.

Press the mixture into the prepared baking tray, but don't push the mixture down too tightly; you want the dough to hold together in the tray, but not be packed so tightly that the biscuits will be too dense. Use the back of a spoon to gently smooth the surface.

Bake for 30 minutes until golden brown. Cut into 12 even-sized rectangles while still warm and sprinkle with caster sugar. Leave to cool completely.

Biscuits

The Benedict Bar

Makes 20 squares

For a twist on the classic shortbread, we add almonds, butter and honey to it to make our Benedict Bar. We use Greek honey when we make this, but you can use your favourite runny honey instead if you prefer.

For the shortbread
175 g (6 oz) salted butter, plus extra for greasing, at room temperature
100 g (3½ oz/scant ½ cup) caster (superfine) sugar, plus extra to finish
175 g (6 oz/scant 1½ cups) plain (all-purpose) flour

For the topping
500 g (1 lb 2 oz/5 cups) flaked (slivered) almonds
250 g (9 oz) butter
350 g (12 oz) honey

Make the shortbread following the method on page 140, but halfway through the cooking time start making the almond topping. Put the ingredients into a saucepan over a low heat and bring up to a bubble, stirring constantly – it should take about 8 minutes.

When the shortbread is done, remove it from the oven and pour the hot almond honey mixture over it (don't cut it into pieces at this stage), then return the tray to the oven.

Bake for a further 20 minutes or until golden. Remove the shortbread from the oven and leave to cool for 15 minutes before cutting into 20 even-sized squares.

Biscuits

The Breton

Makes 10 biscuits

115 g (4 oz) salted butter, plus extra
   for greasing
65 g (2 oz/generous ¼ cup) demerara
   sugar, plus extra for sprinkling
100 g (3½ oz/generous ¾ cup) plain
   (all-purpose) flour, plus 1 teaspoon
   for dusting

Place all the ingredients into the bowl of a food processor and beat until almost combined; the dough will be the texture of rough breadcrumbs.

Tip the 'almost' dough into a large mixing bowl. Use your hands to bring it all together and continue kneading until you have a smooth dough.

Transfer the dough on to a sheet of baking parchment and roll the dough into a log with a 5 cm (2 inch) diameter.

Sprinkle the baking parchment with some demerara sugar and roll the log in the sugar to coat it. Wrap the paper around the log and twist the ends to secure, then chill in the fridge for 30 minutes.

While the dough is chilling, preheat the oven to 180°C (350°F/Gas 4) and butter and flour a baking tray. Remove the paper wrapping from the chilled dough and cut the log into 1 cm- (½ in-) thick biscuits.

Lay the biscuits on the prepared baking tray and bake for 35 minutes or until they are a lovely golden brown colour. Allow to cool on a rack.

Biscuits

Sablés with Buttercream

Makes 10 biscuits

220 g (8 oz) salted butter
130 g (4½ oz/1 cup) icing
   (confectioners') sugar, plus extra
   to finish
2 large eggs
2 egg yolks
350 g (12 oz/generous 2¾ cups)
   plain (all-purpose) flour, plus extra
   for dusting

For the filling
150 g (5 oz) unsalted butter
70 g (2½ oz/generous ½ cup) icing
   (confectioners') sugar

Make the biscuits by creaming the butter and icing sugar together in a food processor. Beat in the eggs and egg yolks, then sift in the flour and continue to beat until you have a smooth, sticky dough.

Remove the dough from the bowl and wrap in cling film (plastic wrap). Chill in the fridge for at least 2 hours, or preferably overnight.

Preheat the oven to 160°C (320°F/Gas 3) and flour your work surface. Roll out the chilled dough to 5 mm (¼ in) thick. Using an 8 cm (3 in) plain round pastry cutter, cut out 10 rounds. Re-roll the dough from time to time if necessary.

Place the rounds 3 cm (1 in) apart on a greased and lined baking tray and bake for 10 minutes until they are golden in colour. Allow to cool completely on a wire rack.

While the biscuits are cooling, make the buttercream filling by whisking the butter and icing sugar together until you have a light, creamy icing. Spread the buttercream on to half of the cooled biscuits, then top each one with another biscuit to make a sandwich. Sift icing sugar over all the filled biscuits and serve with a cup of Barry's Gold Blend tea!

Supper

6

THE NIGHT AHEAD

Around 5 o'clock comes a hiatus that is used to take stock and prepare for the night ahead. The counters are cleared and wines brought out and tasted, the boards changed and the lights are dimmed. The cured meats are massaged, the cheeses scraped and the raclette machine fired up. Most importantly, the leg of jamón is prepared and, if needs be, a new one is opened up. By 6 o'clock the change of mood outside on the pavements of Soho is tangible: people dart hither and thither, meeting friends after work, looking for places to settle for a drink or bite to eat.

A less elaborate affair than dinner, supper is nonetheless an important part of the Fernandez & Wells repertoire: where platters of cured meats and cheeses take centre stage, and of course wine, with huge care taken to ensure that it complements the food we serve.

Soups

Onion soup

Serves 6

We used to make this onion soup every so often at Lexington Street, but the industrial quantity of sliced onions required came at the cost of many tears and the smell seemed to permeate everyone's clothes for days. Still, it remains a terrific recipe and something all of us make at home.

6 tablespoons olive oil
3 tablespoons salted butter
10 large white onions, sliced
10 garlic cloves, peeled and
    finely chopped
1 litre (34 fl oz) dry white wine
1 tablespoon dark muscovado sugar
2 litres (68 fl oz) chicken stock
2 bay leaves
small bunch thyme
sea salt and freshly ground
    black pepper
day-old sourdough bread, to serve
goats' cheese (such a charolais,
    available from Mons at Borough
    Market), to serve (optional)

In a large saucepan, gently heat the olive oil, then add the butter and allow it to melt. Add the onions and garlic, and cook for 30 minutes or until the onions are soft and brown. They need to be well caramelised as this will give the soup its distinctive flavour.

Meanwhile, in a separate saucepan gently heat the wine until it starts to bubble and simmer until it has reduced by about a third. This evaporates the alcohol, removing a harshness that can influence the taste of the final soup.

Sprinkle the sugar into the pan of caramelised onions, pour in the reduced wine and cook through for 5 minutes. Add the stock, bay leaves and the thyme, and cook gently over a low heat for a further 20 minutes. Add the salt to taste and a good grind of black pepper.

Serve in warmed bowls with a chunk of sourdough baguette and a herby piece of dry goats' cheese scattered into the bowls.

Soups

Roasted Tomato and Harissa Soup

Serves 4

1.5 kg (3 lb 5 oz) very ripe tomatoes
4 tablespoons olive oil
6 garlic cloves, peeled and lightly
    crushed with the back of a knife
1 Spanish onion, peeled and cut
    into chunks
250 ml (8½ fl oz) red wine
    (preferably Rioja)
1 teaspoon dark soft brown sugar
1 tablespoon harissa paste
    (see page 225)
3 teaspoons sea salt
1 litre (34 fl oz) vegetable stock
crusty bread, to serve

We often make this soup with the 'gone soft' heritage tomatoes that we have lying around. There is absolutely nothing fancy about this recipe – it is a simple throw-it-all-together rustic soup and all the better for it.

Preheat the oven to 180°C (350°F/Gas 4). Toss the tomatoes in the olive oil in a large bowl and gently squeeze them with your hand until the tomatoes start to break up.

Tip the tomatoes into a large roasting tray, add the garlic cloves, onion, wine, sugar, harissa and 1 teaspoon of the salt, and mix everything to combine. Bake for approximately 50 minutes or until some of the tomatoes start to caramelise a little at the edges.

Remove the tomatoes from the oven and stir in the rest of the salt. Carefully transfer the roasted tomato mixture into a food processor, pour in the stock and blitz until smooth. You may need to do this in batches depending on the size of your food processor.

Pour the soup into a large saucepan and warm back through over a gentle heat. Season to taste (if needed) and serve with a drizzle of olive oil and some crusty bread.

Soups

Marrakechi Shepherds' Mountain Soup

Serves 4

400 g (14 oz) butternut squash,
    peeled and cut into cubes
300 ml (10 fl oz) olive oil
4 garlic cloves, roughly chopped
400 g (14 oz) potatoes, peeled and
    cut into cubes
1.5 litres (3 pints 3 fl oz) hot
    vegetable stock
450 g (1 lb) spinach leaves
4 tablespoons chopped mint
4 tablespoons chopped coriander
    (cilantro)
350 g (12 oz) cooked couscous
salt and freshly ground black pepper

Preheat the oven to 200°C (400°F/Gas 6). Scatter the butternut squash evenly in a baking tray and pour half of the olive oil over it. Roast the squash for 10–15 minutes or until tender. Remove from the oven and set aside.

Heat the remaining oil in a large saucepan over a high heat (but do not allow it to smoke), add the garlic and fry for 1 minute.

Add the potato and cook for another 2 minutes, then pour in the stock, reduce the heat and cook for 15 minutes. Spoon the roasted squash into the pan and, if you have a hand-held blender, blend everything together until smooth. Alternatively, put the squash into a food processor, then carefully pour or ladle in the soup and blitz until smooth. Pour the soup back into the pan and warm back through over a gentle heat.

Stir in the spinach leaves, herbs and the couscous. Season to taste and serve.

Soups

Salmorejo

6 × 400 g (14 oz) tins tomatoes
4 garlic cloves, peeled
½ cucumber, chopped
1½ tablespoons harissa paste
   (see page 225)
2 small onions, peeled and sliced
½ red (bell) pepper, deseeded
   and chopped
½ green (bell) pepper, deseeded
   and chopped
3 tablespoons sherry vinegar
sea salt and freshly ground
   black pepper
olive oil, to serve
finely chopped parsley, to serve
crusty bread, to serve

When we started out, Marcelo made a genuine gazpacho using a recipe passed down from his great-grandmother. Over time, this changed to salmorejo, a thicker, creamier version of gazpacho with origins in the city of Cordoba. An uncooked soup served cold, it is easy to make and comes into its own during the hot summer months. In this version that we make at Fernandez & Wells, we add harissa paste to give it an extra bit of a punch.

Blend all the ingredients together in a food processor until smooth. You will need to do this in batches; pour the soup into a large bowl before blending the next batch.

Mix in a little cold water to loosen the soup, season to taste, cover and chill overnight.

Decant into ice-cold bowls – you can stand each bowl on a plate of crushed ice – and serve with a good drizzle of olive oil, a little chopped parsley and a hunk of crusty bread

Pans

Taktouka

Serves 2

This spicy cooked tomato and pepper salad is the Moroccan version of a dish found in various guises throughout the Middle East and North Africa. Ours comes thanks to Dee's culinary adventures in Morocco, where it is a staple supper dish. As our cooked meals are designed around our grills, this comes served in an individual pan with an egg or two and crusty bread.

1 green (bell) pepper
1 yellow (bell) pepper
1 red (bell) pepper
150 ml (5 fl oz) olive oil
½ teaspoon ground coriander
   (cilantro)
½ teaspoon ground ginger
1 teaspoon ground cinnamon
2 teaspoons ground cumin
3 garlic cloves, finely chopped
1 × 400 g (14 oz) tin chopped
   tomatoes
2 tablespoons harissa paste
   (see page 225)
1 teaspoon soft light brown sugar
1 teaspoon sea salt
2 tablespoons chopped coriander
   (cilantro) leaves
4 large eggs
crusty bread, to serve

For the dressing
2 tablespoons chopped mint leaves
75 ml (2½ fl oz) olive oil

Preheat the oven to 240°C (465°F/Gas 9). Mix together the dressing ingredients in a small bowl or jug and set aside.

Put all 3 peppers into a roasting tin and roast in the oven for 40 minutes until soft and ready to collapse. Alternatively, cook the peppers in a dry (don't add any oil) griddle pan (ribbed skillet) on a very high temperature, turning the them frequently.

Transfer the peppers to a large plastic food bag, seal the bag to trap in the heat and leave for 15 minutes to loosen their skins. Remove the peppers from the bag then peel, halve and deseed them.

Pour the oil into a heavy-based, high-sided frying pan (skillet) over a medium heat. When hot, add the ground coriander, ginger, cinnamon, cumin and garlic. Cook for 30 seconds and then add the tomatoes, harissa, sugar and salt. Simmer gently over a low heat for 20 minutes.

Meanwhile, cut the peppers into 2 cm (¾ in) pieces. Add them to the pan and cook for a further 5 minutes. Fold in the chopped coriander.

Break the eggs into the taktouka; cover and cook for approximately 3 minutes or until the eggs are cooked to your liking – we like the whites cooked but the yolks still nice and runny.

Divide the taktouka between 2 plates, with 2 eggs each and drizzle over the dressing to finish. Serve immediately with some crusty bread.

Chorizo with Lentils

Serves 4 as a starter

This rich, smoky dish is made even better by using top quality ingredients; we use Alejandro chorizo, which is produced in La Rioja region in Spain, Rioja wine and the Spanish Navarrico lentils, which you can buy ready-cooked, but you can use others if you prefer.

150 ml (5 fl oz) extra-virgin
olive oil, plus extra to serve
500 g (1 lb 2 oz) chorizo
1 large onion, finely chopped
4 garlic cloves, crushed
1 teaspoon paprika
350 ml (12 fl oz) red wine
1 kg (2 lb 3 oz) tinned chopped
tomatoes
1 teaspoon soft brown sugar
250 g (9 oz) cooked lentils
salt and freshly ground black pepper
3 tablespoons flat-leaf parsley leaves,
chopped
1 tablespoon harissa paste
(see page 225), to serve

Heat the olive oil in a heavy-based frying pan (skillet) over a medium heat.

Add the chorizo to the pan and cook for 5 minutes, then remove with a slotted spoon to a plate and keep to one side.

Turn the heat down to low and fry the onion in the same pan for about 5 minutes until translucent but not browned. Add the garlic and fry for another 3 minutes.

Stir in the paprika and cook for a further 2 minutes. Pour in the red wine and cook for 3 minutes more. Add the tomatoes and sugar, and cook for another 5 minutes before adding the lentils. Cook for a final 20 minutes or so until the sauce has thickened.

Stir through the parsley and transfer the lentils to a serving dish. Drizzle over some olive oil and top with the harissa paste. Serve hot with the chorizo and a glass of Rioja.

Pans

Menemen

Serves 4

This is a traditional Turkish dish eaten at breakfast with crusty bread and olive oil, and can be served with chopped hard-boiled eggs. We love the tangy taste of unpasteurised barrel-aged feta in this recipe, but you can use regular feta if you like.

50 ml (2 fl oz) olive oil
1 small onion, finely sliced
2 garlic cloves, minced
1 teaspoon ground cinnamon
½ teaspoon chilli powder
1 kg (2 lb 3 oz) tinned chopped
  tomatoes
2 red (bell) peppers, roasted, peeled,
  deseeded and cut into strips
  (see page 165)
4 eggs, whisked
salt to taste
250 g (9 oz) feta
1 tablespoon chopped mint leaves,
  to serve

Heat the oil in a heavy-based frying pan (skillet) and fry the onion on a low heat for 5 minutes. Add the garlic and cook for a further 3 minutes.

Stir through the cinnamon and chilli, then pour in the tomatoes and cook for 20 minutes with the lid on.

Add the red pepper strips and cook for a final 2–3 minutes to heat them though. Taste and add salt as necessary.

Fold in the lightly whisked eggs and gently scramble, or in place of the scrambled eggs, this dish can be served with chopped hard boiled eggs crumbled on top with the feta.

Tip everything into a serving dish, crumble over the feta and sprinkle with the mint to finish.

Pans

Lentils with Pancetta

Serves 4

We use Spanish sweet smoked paprika – pimentón de la Vera, dulce – in this recipe, but you can use any sweet smoked paprika if a Spanish one is difficult to find.

225 g (8 oz/1¼ cups) green or brown lentils or ready-cooked Navarrico lentils (see page 167)
6 tablespoons olive oil
1 head garlic, cloves peeled and thinly sliced
1 onion, finely chopped
1 tablespoon sweet smoked paprika
2 large vine-ripened tomatoes, skinned and chopped
125 ml (4 fl oz) dry white wine
1 tablespoon chopped flat-leaf parsley
1½ teaspoons salt
freshly ground black pepper
8 thick slices pancetta

If using uncooked lentils, rinse them in cold water and drain. Put them in a saucepan, add enough cold water to cover them by 8 cm (3 in) and bring to the boil over a high heat. Reduce the heat and allow the lentils to simmer for about 30 minutes until just tender. Drain and transfer to a bowl, but keep the cooking liquid.

Fry the garlic and onion in the olive oil in a large, high-sided frying pan (skillet) over a medium heat for about 8 minutes. Stir in the paprika, tomatoes and wine, and simmer for 5–6 minutes or until the mixture cooks down into a thick sauce.

Stir the lentils into the sauce with 150 ml (5 fl oz) of the reserved cooking liquid, the chopped parsley, salt and a good grinding of black pepper.

In a separate frying pan, fry the pancetta for 3 minutes on both sides.

Divide the lentils between 4 plates and add 2 slices of pancetta to each dish. Serve immediately.

Pans

Tortilla on a Sourdough Flute

Serves 1

1 large potato, peeled and thinly
  sliced
2 tablespoons olive oil
1 small white onion, thinly sliced
2 eggs, lightly beaten
sea salt
small sourdough flute, to serve
butter, to serve
good-quality tomato ketchup,
  to serve

People speak about a national divide in Spain when it comes to tortilla: to onion or not to onion? We fall into the onion camp. With that established, we keep this tortilla as simple as possible, letting the caramelised onions speak for themselves. Ideally, use a small frying pan (skillet) suitable for a single serving, and serve with Isle of Wight tomato ketchup.

Bring a saucepan of lightly salted water to the boil and cook the potato for 8 minutes. Drain the potato well and allow to steam for a couple of minutes (which helps reduce the water content), then set aside.

Add the oil to a small frying pan (skillet) and heat gently. Add the onion and cook over a low heat for about 10 minutes until the onion starts to soften and then lightly brown. Add the potato and gently fold into the onion.

Pour in the eggs and with a fork spread the potato and onion in the pan evenly. Leave to cook over a medium heat for 5 minutes. Use a spatula to gently loosen the tortilla from the pan. Put a plate face down over the pan and, holding the plate firmly in place, quickly but carefully (don't touch any hot part of the pan) flip the plate and pan over so that the tortilla is now on the plate. Return the tortilla to the pan with the cooked side face up by sliding it from the plate back into the pan. Place the pan back on the heat and cook for a further 4 minutes. Once cooked, transfer the tortilla to another plate.

To serve, split the sourdough flute in half lengthways and butter it. Slice the tortilla in half and lay the pieces on the bottom half of the sourdough. Sprinkle with a good pinch of salt, top with the other half of the sourdough and serve with a dollop of tomato ketchup.

Bowls

Rabbit Stew

Serves 6–8

We first made this shortly after opening at Lexington Street and it was only available to take away. It seemed a natural thing, to try and serve something that we know and loved to eat ourselves, but it clearly was quite a novelty on the streets of Soho.

3 tablespoons plain (all-purpose) flour
1 teaspoon salt, plus extra to season
1 teaspoon freshly ground black pepper, plus extra to season
2 wild (young) rabbits, jointed into 8 pieces
100 ml (3½ fl oz) olive oil
2 onions, coarsely chopped
250 g (9 oz) pancetta
350 g (12 oz) carrots, cut into bite-sized chunks
500 ml (17 fl oz) Breton cider
500 ml (17 fl oz) chicken stock
2 teaspoons dried sage
4 bay leaves
crusty bread, to serve

Preheat the oven to 160°C (320°F/Gas 3). Put the flour into a large mixing bowl and season with some salt and pepper. Stir to combine. Add the rabbit and toss the pieces in the flour to coat everything.

Heat half of the olive oil in a large heavy-based frying pan (skillet) over a medium heat and brown the rabbit pieces, turning occasionally, until they are golden on all sides. You may have to do this in batches. Remove the browned rabbit from the pan with a slotted spoon and transfer it to a casserole.

Add the onions to the same frying pan and sweat gently over a low heat for 5 minutes, then add the pancetta and carrots and cook for a further 5 minutes. Transfer everything to the casserole dish with the rabbit pieces.

Pour the cider into the hot pan and allow it bubble for a few minutes; this will evaporate the alcohol and improve the flavour of the stew. Pour the reduced cider over the rabbit and vegetables. Finally, add the chicken stock, sage and bay leaves to the casserole.

Cover tightly with the lid and cook for approximately 1 hour and 30 minutes until the rabbit is falling off the bone. Adjust the seasoning to taste and serve with some crusty bread.

Bowls

Chicken Tagine with Green Olives

Serves 4

110 ml (3½ fl oz) olive oil
1 Spanish onion, finely chopped
8 chicken thighs, skinned
4 garlic cloves, crushed
2 teaspoons ras el hanout
1 large piece preserved lemon,
    chopped
3 teaspoons chopped coriander
    (cilantro) leaves
125 g (4 oz) pitted green olives
700 ml (23½ fl oz) chicken stock
2 teaspoons chopped flat-leaf parsley
crusty bread or roast potatoes,
    to serve

Heat the olive oil in a large high-sided, heavy-based frying pan (skillet) and add the onion. Cook on a gentle heat for about 5 minutes until translucent.

Add the chicken thighs to the pan and increase the heat slightly. Cook for another 5 minutes, turning occasionally.

Add the garlic, cook for a further 3 minutes, then add the ras el hanout, preserved lemon, coriander and olives.

Pour the chicken stock into the pan so the contents are only just covered – you may not need all of the stock, depending on the size of your pan. Bring to the boil and then reduce the heat to a gentle simmer. Cover and cook for 30 minutes or until the chicken is cooked through.

Sprinkle with the parsley and serve with roast potatoes or crusty bread.

Bowls

Beef with Prunes

Serves 4

6 tablespoons olive oil
1 kg (2 lb 3 oz) chuck steak, cut into
  chunks
2 white onions, peeled
  and sliced
4 garlic cloves, finely chopped
3 teaspoons ras el hanout
3 teaspoons ground coriander
  (cilantro)
1 teaspoon ground cinnamon
1 chilli, deseeded and finely chopped
400 ml (13 fl oz) Rioja red wine
650 g (1 lb 7 oz) chopped tomatoes
500 ml (17 fl oz) water
sea salt and freshly ground black
  pepper
150 g (5 oz) no-soak pitted prunes
½ bunch mint, finely chopped
½ bunch coriander (cilantro),
  finely chopped
boiled or buttery mash potatoes,
  to serve

Heat 1½ tablespoons of the olive oil in a large high-sided, heavy-based frying pan (skillet). Brown the beef in batches over a high heat and transfer to a casserole.

Add another 1½ tablespoons of olive oil to the pan, reduce the heat to medium and cook the onion for 5 minutes. Add the garlic and cook for a further 3 minutes. Sprinkle over the spices and cook, stirring constantly, for another 3 minutes. Finally, add the chilli and cook for 2 minutes, then tip the contents of the pan into the casserole with the beef.

Pour the red wine into the pan to deglaze it, stirring the wine with a wooden spoon to make sure you get all the caramelised bits from the bottom of the pan, which are full of flavour. Reduce for 5 minutes then pour over the meat.

Add the tomatoes and water to the casserole. Season with 2 teaspoons of sea salt and a good grinding of black pepper, and stir the casserole once.

Cover the casserole tightly with the lid and cook in the oven for 2 hours. Check from time to time that the dish is not drying out and if it looks like it is add a bit more water.

Remove from the oven and stir in the prunes and fresh herbs. Replace the lid and allow to stand for 15 minutes before serving. Serve with boiled or buttery mash potatoes.

Bowls

Puré de Patatas with Tacos de Jamón

Serves 4

1.2 kg (2 lb 10 oz) good quality floury potatoes (such as King Edward), halved
2 bay leaves
4 tablespoons salted butter, plus extra to serve
1 level teaspoon sea salt
250 g (9 oz) ibérico jamón, cut into small cubes

When yet another magnificent leg of our aged jamón ibérico is sliced down virtually to the bone, the tail end bits are cut off and chopped into small cubes or thick slices, and served in a small bowl. These 'tacos de jamón', as they are known in Spain, are a treat added to mashed potato.

Fill a large saucepan with cold water, add the potatoes and the bay leaves and cover. Bring to the boil, reduce the heat to a simmer and cook the potatoes for 15 minutes or until a sharp knife passes through the potatoes easily. Drain and remove the bay leaves.

Push each potato through a potato ricer into a large bowl. Meanwhile, heat the butter in a small pan until melted, then add it to the potatoes. Mash through with a fork and finally mix in the salt.

Spoon the potatoes on to four warm plates, throw over the jamón pieces and an extra knob of butter and serve immediately.

Bowls

Zaalouk

Serves 4

The key to this simple Moroccan dish is to really blacken the aubergines (eggplants) to give it a delicious smoky grilled flavour. Essentially a cooked salad of aubergines, tomatoes, garlic, olive oil and spices, it is delicious simply spread on bread or toast. It is also good with yoghurt and is a great partner of baked lamb.

2 large aubergines (eggplants)
1 tablespoon lemon juice
120 ml (4 fl oz) olive oil
500 g (1 lb 2 oz) tomatoes, skinned, deseeded and diced
½ level teaspoon soft brown sugar
3 garlic cloves, crushed
1 teaspoon salt
1 teaspoon ground cumin
½ teaspoon ground coriander (cilantro) seeds
½ teaspoon chilli powder
2 tablespoons chopped coriander (cilantro) leaves
crusty bread, to serve

Preheat the oven to 190°C (375°F/Gas 5).

Prick the aubergines all over with a fork or the tip of a sharp knife, place on a baking tray and bake for 30 minutes until they have almost collapsed.

Allow the the aubergines to become cool enough to handle, then, while they're still warm, peel off the skin of one (or both, depending on what you prefer). Drain away any excess liquid using a colander, then tip the aubergines into a large bowl. Sprinkle them with the lemon juice and leave for 15 minutes, then chop vigorously until they're finely diced.

Heat the olive oil in a large high-sided, heavy-based frying pan (skillet) over a medium heat. Add the tomatoes, sugar, garlic, salt and dried spices to the pan, reduce the heat, and cook gently for 15 minutes.

Stir in the fresh coriander and chopped aubergines, and combine thoroughly. Serve with slices of crusty bread.

Plates

Hummus bi Tahini

Serves 2–4

Hummus means 'chickpea' in Arabic, and mixed with sesame paste (or tahini), lemon juice, salt and garlic, this humble pulse becomes everyone's favourite healthy dip. Serve with a drizzle of olive oil and sourdough toast.

250 g (9 oz) tin chickpeas
60 ml (2 fl oz) lemon juice
3 garlic cloves, crushed
1 teaspoon harissa paste
  (see page 225)
1 teaspoon chopped mint leaves
½ teaspoon ground cumin
1 teaspoon salt
150 ml (5 fl oz) tahini paste
4 tablespoons light olive oil, plus
  extra to serve
sea salt and freshly ground black
  pepper
sprinkle of paprika, to serve
sourdough toast, to serve

Drain the chickpeas in a colander and rinse them in cold water.

Place the chickpeas along with the remaining ingredients in a food processor and blitz until you have a smooth, creamy paste. Season to taste and add a sprinkle of paprika. Serve with sourdough toast and a glug of olive oil.

Plates

Caponata

Serves 4

4 large aubergines (eggplants),
   chopped into 2 cm (¾ in) cubes
1 teaspoon salt, plus extra for
   seasoning
110 ml (3½ fl oz) olive oil
1 onion, diced
3 garlic cloves, crushed
500 g (1 lb 2 oz) chopped tomatoes
   (fresh or tinned)
125 g (4 oz) pitted Sicilian
   green olives
6 tablespoons drained capers
25 ml (1 fl oz) red wine vinegar
1½ teaspoons soft brown sugar
2 tablespoons chopped flat-leaf
   parsley
freshly ground black pepper

Most people associate this dish with Sicily, although the word itself may be of Catalan origin. A vegetable stew, based on aubergines (eggplants), with tomatoes, onions, capers and sugar as well as vinegar to give it its distinctive sweet/sour flavour, it can be served cold or warm as a side dish.

Place the aubergine pieces in a colander over a large bowl and sprinkle with the salt. Leave for 30 minutes to allow the salt to draw out the water from the aubergine, then rinse thoroughly and pat dry with paper towels.

Heat the oil in a large high-sided, heavy-based frying pan (skillet) over a medium heat and brown the aubergine pieces all over. Remove them from the pan with a slotted spoon and leave to rest on some kitchen paper.

Add the onion to the same pan and cook on a gentle heat for about 5 minutes until translucent. Add the garlic and cook for a further 3 minutes.

Stir the tomatoes and olives into the pan and season with salt and pepper, to taste. Simmer on a gentle heat for 20 minutes.

Meanwhile, mix the capers, vinegar and sugar together in a bowl. Put the aubergine back into the pan with the tomatoes and fold in the caper mix. Add the chopped parsley, check the seasoning and serve.

Plates

White Beans, Black Pudding and Egg

Serves 4

2 shallots, finely chopped

3 garlic cloves, peeled and crushed
  with the back of a knife

2 tablespoons salted butter

250 ml (8½ fl oz) dry white wine

350 g (12 oz) tinned haricot beans

350 g (12 oz) tinned cannellini
  beans

300 ml (10 fl oz) chicken stock

4 sage leaves, finely chopped

300 ml (10 fl oz) double
  (heavy) cream

4 × 2 cm- (¾ in-) thick slices Grants
  of Speyside or any good-quality
  black pudding

1 tablespoon olive oil

4 eggs

½ teaspoon sea salt

In a large high-sided frying pan (skillet), fry the shallots and garlic in 1 tablespoon of the butter over a low heat for 5–7 minutes until the shallots are nicely softened. Add the white wine and cook for 5 minutes, then add the haricot and cannellini beans and fold through. Pour in the stock and add the sage leaves. Cook for 10 minutes, then stir in the cream and simmer for 3 minutes. Remove from the heat but cover to keep the beans hot.

In a separate frying pan, fry the black pudding in the olive oil over a medium heat for 4 minutes on each side. Transfer to a plate and cover to keep warm.

Put the remaining butter in the frying pan, turn the heat to high and, once melted, crack the eggs into the pan. Just as the eggs are starting to turn white, fold each side of the eggs over the yolks and flip them over one by one. Fry for just 1 minute more; the eggs whites will cook quickly but the yolks will still be runny inside.

Divide the beans between 4 plates and top each one with a slice of black pudding and a fried egg and sprinkle with the salt.

Kidneys with Garlic, Parsley and Butter

Serves 1

Relatively cheap, easy to prepare and very nourishing, lamb's kidneys are great for a quick breakfast or light supper. Despite people's reticence towards offal, such tasty morsels have been making a comeback on menus; sometimes 'devilled', meaning with a spicy mustard sauce, and served on toast. We love this simple version, which goes equally well with a cup of tea or a glass of red wine, such as a Cabernet Franc from Bourgueil in the Loire Valley.

2 lamb's kidneys
2 tablespoons salted butter
2 tablespoons finely chopped
    flat-leaf parsley
sea salt and freshly ground black
    pepper
3 garlic cloves, finely chopped
200 g (7 oz) white cabbage,
    finely shredded
1 teaspoon Dijon mustard

Prepare the kidneys by removing the clear membrane that covers them, then cut them in half and cut out the white core.

Add half a tablespoon of the butter to a frying pan (skillet) and heat until it has just melted and is beginning to froth. Add the kidneys and cook them gently over a medium heat for 2 minutes on each side until cooked through. Add the parsley and stir to combine. Season to taste.

Remove the kidneys from the pan and keep them warm to one side. Put the rest of the butter into the pan and once melted add the garlic and fry for 2 minutes.

Add the white cabbage, mustard and a pinch of salt, then add a drop of hot water and cook on a very high heat for 5 minutes. Serve hot straight from the pan, with the kidneys.

Ibérico Chop with Fried Leeks

Serves 2

With the 24-month cured jamón ibérico de bellota from Juan Pedro Domecq, one of our core products, it's hardly surprising that when a juicy Ibérico chop is in the offing, we're quick to partake of that too. It is the diet of roots and acorns from foraging on the dehesa – the oak tree-studded pasturelands of southern Spain – that makes these Iberian pigs so special and gives the meat this extra depth of flavour and nuttiness.

2 Ibérico pork chops
1 tablespoon olive oil
2 leeks, sliced
1 tablespoon butter
sea salt and freshly ground
  black pepper
mash potatoes, to serve (optional)

For the marinade
4 tablespoons olive oil
2 sprigs thyme

Make the marinade by putting the olive oil and thyme into a shallow dish big enough to hold the chops, then add the meat. Turn the chops over in the marinade a few times to cover all sides, then leave for at least 2 hours (or preferably overnight) in the fridge.

Remove the chops from the marinade and season well. Heat a griddle pan (ribbed skillet) over a high heat and lay the chops in the pan. Fry for about 5 minutes until browned, then flip over and brown the other side for 3–5 minutes.

Remove the chops from the pan and leave to rest. Meanwhile, add the oil to the pan and throw on the leeks. Toss for 5 minutes until softened and then add the butter. Serve on a warm plate with the chops and buttery mash potatoes, if you like.

Plates

Onglet with Fried Onion and Mushrooms

Serves 1

1 tablespoon butter
1 × 250 g (9 oz) onglet steak
½ Spanish onion, thinly sliced
100 g (3½ oz) mushrooms
sliced sourdough bread, to serve
salt

Quite common in France, onglet is a cut of beef taken from the diaphragm of a heifer. Less known in Britain, hence fairly cheap, it is called 'skirt' and needs to be prepared well, making sure that the sinews are removed by your butcher. Once that has been done, it must be cooked rare and has great depth of flavour.

Heat a frying pan (skillet) over a high heat until it is hot. Add half a tablespoon of the butter and let it sizzle and turn brown.

Lay the onglet in the pan and fry it for 2 minutes on each side. Remove from the pan and allow it to rest on a plate.

Lower the heat and add the rest of the butter to the pan. Fry the onion for 5–10 minutes until it softens and is lightly browned. Add in the mushrooms and cook for 5 more minutes.

Serve the onglet with the onion and mushrooms, a good pinch of salt and some slices of fresh sourdough.

Potato, Artichoke and Jamón

Serves 4

This is a quick and easy light lunch or supper dish, made special by the addition of some jamón.

350 g (12 oz) potatoes (preferably King Edward), peeled
2 bay leaves
1 teaspoon sea salt
juice of 1 lemon
1 tablespoon salted butter
4 Roman-style artichoke hearts that are widely available in super-markets and delicatessens
60 g (2 oz) jamón, thinly sliced
freshly ground black pepper

Put the potatoes in a large saucepan with just enough water to cover them. Add the bay leaves, half of the salt and half of the lemon juice. Bring to the boil and then cook the potatoes for 20 minutes until they start to break up. Drain the potatoes well in a colander, then give the colander a little shake to make the potatoes floury. Cover to keep warm and set to one side.

Add the butter to a frying pan (skillet), melt it over a medium heat and allow it to froth gently for 30 seconds. Add the artichokes and fry for 6 minutes, turning constantly. Squeeze the remaining lemon juice over the artichokes then transfer them to a warm serving plate. Put the potatoes on to the plate with the artichokes and sprinkle over the remaining salt. Season with the pepper and top the dish with the jamón.

Cheese

At Fernandez & Wells we offer a wide variety of products from around Britain and Europe, all of which are a genuine reflection of our own tastes, but with Fernandez in the name we are inevitably going to be predisposed towards all things Spanish.

So, from the start, it was always expected we would serve manchego, that most ubiquitous of Spanish cheeses from La Mancha, the land of Don Quixote. Jorge, however, harboured strong reservations about manchego's ability to travel well, perhaps because of his experience of the multitude of mediocre examples generally available locally. Our initial thought was to search for an alternative cheese made nearer to home; this came in the form of Berkswell – a hard ewe's milk cheese with a deliciously nutty, rich flavour and often a slightly grainy texture. But, as we have become more established, suppliers have increasingly sought us out with samples of manchego to evaluate; and we still had a nagging feeling that we should have a manchego on our list. It was only when our Spanish supplier of jamón iberico, Juan Pedro Domecq, introduced us to a recommended producer of manchego that we both felt we'd found something that was close to satisfying Jorge's requirements. The gran reserva manchego from Dehesa de Los Llanos was indeed exceptional – so much so it won top prize in the 2012 World Cheese Awards and shortly thereafter they promptly ran out of all their aged stock. Thankfully, over time, this has been replenished.

What this also demonstrates is the painstaking and time consuming way in which many of these artisanal products are made; if it takes nine months to age a cheese, then nine months it has to be.

A company that epitomises this approach is Neal's Yard Dairy, a 'sister' company to Monmouth Coffee by way of geographical location, family connection and ethos. Their range of farmhouse cheeses from the British Isles is unsurpassed, carefully tended and matured so they are sold perfectly ready for consumption. It is no surprise that some of the classics – the cow's milk Montgomery's Cheddar, Duckett's Caerphilly and Irish Coolea; the ewe's milk Berkswell and Wigmore; and the goat's milk Dorstone and Tymsboro – were on the Fernandez & Wells counter right from the start.

These types of cheese lend themselves to being cut with a knife on a wooden block and eaten as you might at a market stall, with bread or on their own with a glass of beer or wine.

Another cheese that was with us from the early days was Ossau-Iraty, a sheep's milk variety of ancient origin from the Basque country in south-western France. Although much better known now, it was then quite a rarity and was brought to us by Jon Thrupp, who worked for Hervé Mons, a renowned French 'affineur', skilled in the art of ageing cheese. Mons Cheesemongers in London have provided us with some of the best from France over the years.

One cheese that deserves a special mention is the mozzarella di bufala, sourced by Alsion Elliott at the Ham & Cheese Company. From Paestum in Campania, south of Naples, the dairy is one of the last to use unpasteurised milk to make mozzarella, giving it a slight sour tang to offset the usual creaminess. Described as 'other worldly and delicious' when a fresh batch arrives each week, we delight in offering this white

ball 'neat' on its own, served on a small white plate; we watch for the raised eyebrow of a customer new to the experience and take great pleasure seeing their initial suspicion turn to a smile and a big thumbs up.

On the importance of provenance, it was many years before the advent of Fernandez & Wells that I organised a short trip to Piedmont, in northern Italy. The aim was to taste wine, eat truffles and get to know more about a region whose food and wine had huge appeal. I arranged visits to several top producers of Barolo and Dolcetto and booked places to eat. But the day before leaving I realised to my horror that I had failed to book a hotel and a round of last minute calls proved fruitless. I decided to try one of the restaurants in Monforte D'Alba and having explained my predicament was amazed to be offered the use of a private apartment, 'non c'è problema'! We duly arrived late at night, after a long drive from Turin in a very small Fiat. On introducing ourselves at the reception, word was sent and after a short while a tall, quite fearsome looking man appeared holding a large knife, a 'salame', a hunk of cheese, bread and a bottle of wine, as well as a large key. We followed him in the darkness up a winding cobbled street to an old wooden door, which he opened with the large key, and handing us our 'supper', bid us goodnight. We feasted on these simple delights, slept soundly and awoke to open the shutters on one of the most magnificent views over the terracotta roofs of the hilltop town.

Looking back, it was the combination of hospitality and the certainty that those basic timeless products were all that was needed to satisfy us, that stuck with me. And I like to think, when the time came, made it obvious what we should be trying to do at Fernandez & Wells.

Raclette

Raclette is the name of both a cheese and a traditional Swiss dish of melted cheese, which is sizzled until crisp and bubbling under a grill, then scraped (*racler* means 'to scrape' in French) on to a bed of boiled potatoes, and served with cornichons and cured meats. Traditionally, the handsome round of cheese was cut in half and warmed in front of a fire, but ownership of a raclette machine is a more practical option for most people these days. Simple though they are, these machines do need to be maintained and the electrical elements don't take well to the wear and tear of regular use in the shops, as we have found out to our cost. Still, once fired up there's something about the transformative qualities of grilled cheese, bringing instant warmth and smiles to a room, that make it all worthwhile.

Sourcing a good cheese is important, and we get ours from French cheesemongers, Mons, in London's Borough Market. Depending on the season and availability, we always aim to use the best quality raclette, a type which is known as Alpage. This denotes the time of year – spring and summer – when the cows are herded up into the highest pastures to feed on the best grass, mixed with wild flowers and herbs. This fulfils our aim of turning what can be quite a flavourless experience into one with real depth and farmyard presence.

Puddings

Rice Pudding with Orange Peel

Serves 4

butter, for greasing
75 g (2½ oz) pudding rice
3 strips orange peel (use a potato peeler), plus extra for serving
50 g (2 oz/¼ cup) caster (superfine) sugar
650 ml (22 fl oz) unpasteurised or whole (full-fat) milk
½ teaspoon ground cinnamon
blackberry jam, for serving (optional)
cream, for serving (optional)

One of those simple dishes that falls into the comfort food bracket, rice pudding can be eaten at virtually any time of day or night. With this in mind, Jorge's mother made sure there was always a large bowl of it in the fridge to ensure that at least something was eaten after a long night out. We also associate it with the little metal or terracotta pots, containing creamy rice pudding sprinkled with cinnamon, you see stacked in shop fridges in Greece. The orange peel in this version contains healthy oils and adds a touch of sunny citrus flavour.

Preheat the oven to 160°C (320°F/Gas 3) and grease a 15 × 25 × 8 cm (6 × 10 × 3 in) ovenproof dish with a little butter.

Combine the rice, orange peel, sugar and milk together in a bowl, then pour the mixture into the prepared dish. Sprinkle the cinnamon over the top and bake in the oven for 2½ hours. Serve with a dollop of blackberry jam and a glug of cream, if you like, or simply decorate with orange peel.

Puddings

Blood Oranges with Cinnamon Syrup

Serves 4

4 blood oranges, peeled and broken
  into individual segments
500 g (1 lb 2 oz) ricotta
zest of ½ lemon
1 tablespoon icing (confectioners')
  sugar, sifted
sprig of mint, to serve

For the syrup
300 ml (10 fl oz) water
150 g (5 oz/⅔ cup) caster
  (superfine) sugar
½ teaspoon ground cinnamon

Make the syrup by putting all the syrup ingredients into a medium saucepan over a high heat. Bring the liquid to the boil and boil for 10 minutes or until the syrup has thickened and will coat the back of a spoon.

Pour the syrup over the orange segments in a bowl and leave to cool. Meanwhile, in a separate bowl, gently combine the ricotta, lemon zest and icing sugar.

Arrange the oranges on 4 small plates and add a tablespoon of the ricotta mixture into the middle of each plate. Serve with a sprig of mint.

Puddings

Figs with Chocolate and Mascarpone

Serves 4

You can buy figs out of season, but they tend to be very firm, so baking them, like in this recipe, works wonderfully. However, if you can get them in season when they are soft and perfectly ripe, then you can make this with fresh figs warmed simply by the summer sun.

8 ripe figs (in-season are best)
100 g (3½ oz) dark (bittersweet)
  chocolate, broken into pieces
175 ml (6 fl oz) double (heavy) cream
1 teaspoon rum
250 g (9 oz) mascarpone
50 g (2 oz/scant ½ cup) icing
  (confectioners') sugar, sifted
30 g (1 oz) salted pistachios,
  shelled and chopped (optional)

Cut each fig vertically twice, but not quite through to the bottom, so that you have 4 pieces still held together at the base of the fig. If they are not perfectly ripe, preheat the oven to 180°C (350°F/Gas 4), then place the figs on to a baking tray and bake for 20 minutes.

Melt the chocolate in a medium heatproof bowl sat over a saucepan of gently simmering water – make sure the bottom of the bowl isn't touching the water. Remove the bowl from the pan and sit it on a tea towel (dish towel) on the worktop. Pour in the cream and then the rum, stirring all the time.

In a separate bowl, combine the mascarpone with the icing sugar.

Place 2 figs on to each plate and spoon over a tablespoon of the chocolate sauce. Serve with a generous dollop of the mascarpone and, if you like, a sprinkling of chopped pistachios.

Wine

7

FOR THE TASTEBUDS

Wine was always going to be part of the Fernandez & Wells offer, not least because I had a considerable amount of it to sell. Owning a house in rural France, I came to know some winemakers and as a sideline began to import cases to sell to friends and other 'amateurs'. Additions to the list of 'Rick's Wines' came from Italy and Spain, and enthusiasm for one particular Spanish vineyard resulted in a purchase of 100 cases, a quantity which could not be easily be diminished by home consumption should the need arise! Fortunately this wine, Quinta Sardonia from Sardón del Duero, was to become an early favourite of Fernandez & Wells' customers at Lexington Street.

Wine

If there is a guiding principle concerning the wine at Fernandez & Wells it is that as far as possible it should taste authentic; that's to say it is representative of the place it is from. It is no coincidence that a large proportion of the wines on the list are organic, as winemakers seeking quality in general work hard at minimal intervention. Likewise, the trend towards so-called 'natural' wines is to be encouraged, with some really exciting examples of 'terroir' posing a strong argument against the commercial homogeneity of much modern winemaking.

Another related issue is that of alcohol content. There is evidence to suggest that the best organic and biodynamic wines appear to reach maturity at lower potential alcohol levels than those farmed using chemicals. While consumers have grown to expect higher and higher levels of alcohol in wine, with 14 and 15 per cent fairly standard, the preference at Fernandez & Wells is for more restraint. That does not, however, exclude character and wines are chosen as much to complement the food as to be enjoyed on their own.

For Jorge, early experiences of the taste of wine were not entirely flattering. In a day-to-day sense, wine with meals at home was often watered down with La Casera, a popular Spanish brand of soda. On visits to Los Picos mountains and walks with Uncle Daniel, rough red wine came in the form of a 'leathery tasting squirt' from la bota, the traditional wine or water vessel slung over the shoulder to keep it cool.

My interest in and love of wine began at the age of about 15 or 16, when an enlightened schoolmaster set up a wine club to educate young palates and pass on his undoubted knowledge and enthusiasm for the subject. His actual subject was chemistry, which no doubt lent some academic credibility to an enterprise that would surely not readily slip by the guardians of moral rectitude in today's schools. But in our eyes this was never just an excuse for an illicit booze up. Rather, it opened up a whole new world with its own vocabulary of tastes and smells as well as exotic names, which were recorded in notebooks at each meeting. Some, like Corton and Montrachet, were held in such awe they could be used tactically as an instant distraction from any difficulties that may have arisen over chemistry homework.

Other inspirations included Oddbins stores, in their earliest incarnation, when the name actually reflected the small parcels of treasures one might find from previously unheard of regions and appellations. A similar ethos pervaded La Vigneronne in South Kensington, where Liz and Mike Berry forged their own path in introducing the wines of Languedoc in particular, via wonderfully eclectic tastings in the cellar of their shop.

Sadly, the time-consuming paperwork attached to importing wine, plus the costs of duty, shipping, storage and delivery etc., put paid to the ideal of continuing to list wines chosen from individual producers and brought in ourselves. The challenge is therefore to find like-minded suppliers from which to taste and select for the Fernandez & Wells list.

For various reasons it was decided to limit the wine selection to Europe. While I am a huge fan of wines from all around the globe, and living here in Britain we are lucky to have an almost unique diversity of wines available, the combination of tradition and innovation on our doorstep means there's more than enough to excite the palate when choosing the 30 or so wines on the Fernandez & Wells list. Above all, it seems to me that European wines tend to be great food wines and they go particularly well with the simple, quality fare that we aim to serve.

When it comes to matching food and wines, as a starting point something that may seem obvious but is often overlooked is what people drink where the food is produced. Hence, if it's a goats' cheese produced in central France, you might look at the local wine that accompanies it, which would almost certainly be a sauvignon blanc, like that of Menetou-Salon, not far from the famous village of Sancerre. In the same vein, a good place to start in finding a suitable match for a well-matured manchego, made from ewe's milk, might be from where the cheese originated, La Mancha. A fruity, medium-bodied tempranillo with its characteristic dry finish, for example, could be the popular local choice. If some of our amazing Tuscan charcuterie comes from the village of Montalcino, then why go further than the red sangiovese wines of the area, some of which have a great capacity to improve with age? That doesn't mean to say that a wine from Marcillac in the Lot Valley in south-west France, made from the mansois grape, and which happens to be a superb foil to charcuterie should be overlooked. Choosing a wine to match our wonderful aged Jamón Ibérico is always an enjoyable task and I find depends a lot on the occasion and season. The jamón is always served at room temperature but on warmer summer days it seems fitting to pair with a chilled glass of bone dry Fino or Manzanilla sherry. In winter months it might feel more appropriate to match the deep, nutty flavours of the acorn-rich fat with a red Rioja or Ribeira del Duero, or if you're feeling like a bit of sparkle, a glass of Cava or champagne can hit the spot. And just to throw in another option, there's something wonderful about a simple glass or two of cold beer with a plate of the finest cured meat there is.

But in the end there are no rules, and the fun comes in exploring and tasting as you go along, and this is to be encouraged among staff and customers alike. This is also why we have been keen on having all the wines on the list at Fernandez & Wells available by the glass, switching them on a regular basis, so regulars can make their own minds up.

Grilled Octopus

Whenever we have a new item on the menu, the exploration of wine and food are part and parcel of the training we give our staff. A recent example is the grilled octopus – tender juicy tentacles grilled and served with sea salt, a slice of lemon and lightly toasted sourdough bread.

Having been hauled out of the sea off the coast of Galicia in north-western Spain, a Sameirás blanco we have from Ribeiro Galicia would be a likely match to suggest to any customer seeking guidance.

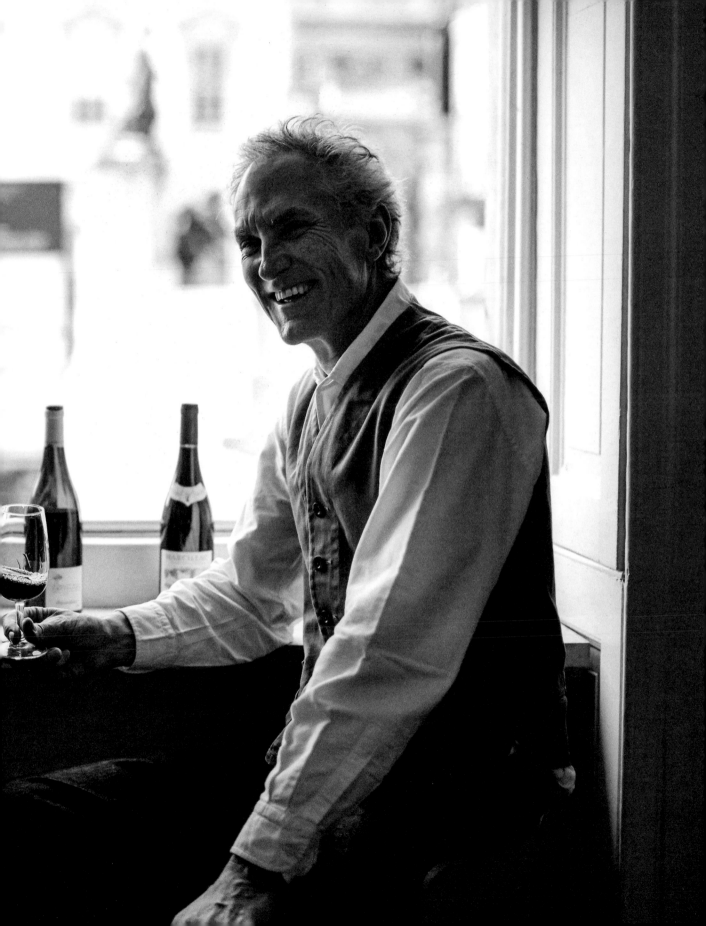

Pickles and Sauces

Harissa

**Makes approximately
550 g (1 lb 3½ oz)**

*400 g (14 oz) red or green chillies,
   halved and deseeded*
2 shallots, finely diced
1 teaspoon dried mint
½ teaspoon ras el hanout
1 tablespoon dried rose petals
200 ml (7 fl oz) olive oil
1 teaspoon sea salt

We make both red and green versions of this hot chilli paste and this recipe works for either colour.

Place all the ingredients into a food processor and blitz until smooth. Transfer to a clean sterilised jar with a good seal. This will keep in the sealed jar in the fridge for up to 3 weeks.

We add this paste to oil and drizzle over fried eggs (see page 55), stir it into soups (see pages 154–61) and mix it into roasted tomatoes. We even add it to lemon cake with extra mint sometimes!

Sundried Tomato and Green Olive Tapenade

**Makes approximately
600 g (1 lb 5 oz)**

250 g (9 oz) pitted green Greek olives
150 g (5 oz) sundried tomatoes
1 teaspoon sea salt
½ teaspoon dried mint
½ teaspoon dried basil
*200 ml (7 fl oz) olive oil, plus extra
   for the top*

While this is great as a dip or simply spread on toast, we make this tapenade for our sandwiches. Spread thickly between slices of sea salt focaccia, topped with barrel-aged feta, then, toasted under the grill, it makes a tasty vegetarian treat.

Blend all of the ingredients together in a food processor until almost smooth; you want the tapenade to retain a bit of texture. Transfer to a clean sterilised well-sealed jar and top with 5 mm (¼ in) of olive oil. Leave for 2 days before serving. This will keep in the fridge for up to 2 weeks.

Piccalilli

This favourite English version of an Indian pickle or relish is definitely best home made. Packed in jars, the bright yellow chopped and pickled summer vegetables are a ready source of tangy, salty flavour; the perfect foil to English cooked ham, cheese and crusty bread eaten as a ploughman's lunch or in a sandwich. A great store bought example is the one we use made by England Preserves.

4 tablespoons olive oil
1 teaspoon mustard seeds
1 teaspoon cumin seeds
1 teaspoon paprika
1 teaspoon turmeric
1 teaspoon mustard powder
200 ml (7 fl oz) white wine vinegar
4 tablespoons caster (superfine)
    sugar
1 cauliflower head, cut into
    small florets
3 celery sticks, cut into
    1 cm (½ in) pieces
1 white onion, cut into
    1 cm (½ in) pieces
250 g (9 oz) green beans, cut into
    2 cm (¾ in) pieces
1 red (bell) pepper, cut into
    2 cm (¾ in) chunks
2 garlic cloves, thinly sliced
2 bay leaves
250 ml (8½ fl oz) warm water
2 level teaspoons sea salt

Heat the oil in a large heavy-based saucepan over a low heat. Add the mustard and cumin seeds, the paprika, turmeric and mustard powder, and mix into a thick paste. Fry very gently for 3 minutes.

Pour in the vinegar and sugar, and mix with a wooden spoon. Add all of the vegetables, the garlic and the bay leaves and stir to combine. Pour in the water and cook over a low heat for about 15 minutes until the vegetables lose their firmness. Add the salt and stir through again.

Take the saucepan off the heat, cover and leave the piccalilli to cool completely. Spoon the piccalilli into clean sterilised jars with a good seal and place in the fridge. Leave for 7 days before using.

Roasted Garlic with Sourdough

Serves 2

30 garlic cloves
4 tablespoons olive oil
250 g (9 oz) stale sourdough bread
250 ml (8½ fl oz) warm water
1 teaspoon sea salt

Preheat the oven to 150°C (300°F/Gas 2). Toss the whole, unpeeled garlic cloves in a large roasting tin with the oil so that they are all coated. Roast for 1 hour, giving the tray a shake halfway through, until the garlic is completely soft. Remove the tray from the oven and allow the garlic to cool slightly until safe to handle.

In a large bowl, soak the bread in the water for 5 minutes. Meanwhile, squeeze the garlic out of its skins and into a large pestle and mortar. Remove the bread from the water, squeeze it out, then tear it into the pestle and mortar with the garlic and salt. Pound the mixture until well combined and then devour. It will not hang around for too long!

Favourite London Addresses

MARKETS

Spa Terminus Market
A Saturday morning market for great cheeses, cured meats, bread, fruit and vegetables, coffee, wines and more. Including many of the producers listed below.
Dockley Road Industrial Estate,
Dockley Road, London SE16 3SF
www.spa-terminus.co.uk

COFFEE

Coleman Coffee Roasters
www.colemancoffee.com

Has Bean Coffee Ltd
www.hasbean.co.uk

Monmouth Coffee Company
Multiple locations
www.monmouthcoffee.co.uk

CHEESE

La Fromagerie
Excellent cheeses and tempting produce
Multiple locations
www.lafromagerie.co.uk

Mons Cheesemongers
Borough Market
London SE1 1TL
www.mons-cheese.co.uk

Neal's Yard Dairy
Multiple locations
www.nealsyarddairy.co.uk

MEAT

The Ham & Cheese Co.
Multiple locations
www.thehamandcheeseco.com

Jack O'Shea
Great meat including Ibérico chops
65, Regent's Park Road
London NW1 8XD
www.jackoshea.com

Provenance
Village Butcher
33 Kensington Park Road
London W11 2EU
www.provenancebutcher.com

FRUIT AND VEG

Fern Verrow
Organic, biodynamic fruit and vegetables, available at Spa Terminus Market
www.fernverrow.com

WINE

40 Maltby Street
A great wine bar with food
London SE1 3PA
www.40maltbystreet.com

Aubert & Mascoli
Arch 2 Voyager BP
Spa Road
London SE16 4RP
www.aubertandmascoli.com

The Winery
A fantastic wine shop in Maida Vale
4 Clifton Road
London W9 1SS
www.thewineryuk.com

RESTAURANTS AND CAFÉS

Barrafina
Multiple locations
www.barrafina.co.uk

Honey & Co.
25a Warren Street
London W1T 5LZ
www.honeyandco.co.uk

Koya Bar
50 Frith Street
London W1D 4SQ
www.koyabar.co.uk

Moro
34–36 Exmouth Market
London EC1R 4QE
www.moro.co.uk

Ottolenghi
Multiple locations
www.ottolenghi.co.uk

The Palomar
34 Rupert Street
London W1D 6DN
www.thepalomar.co.uk

St. John
26 St John Street
London EC1M 4AY
www.stjohngroup.uk.com

The Towpath Café
42 De Beauvoir Crescent
London N1 5SB

The Sportsman
A truly perfect restaurant in Kent
Faversham Road, Seasalter,
Whitstable, Kent CT5 4BP
www.thesportsmanseasalter.co.uk

FAVOURITE SHOPS

Arthur Beale
194 Shaftesbury Avenue
London WC2H 8JP
www.arthurbeale.co.uk

Labour & Wait
85 Redchurch Street
London E2 7DJ
www.labourandwait.co.uk

Leila's Shop
A café and grocery
15–17 Calvert Avenue
London E2 7JP

Pedlars General Store
128 Talbot Road
London W11 1JA
www.pedlars.co.uk

Old Town
British clothing
Old Town, 49 Bull Street, Holt,
Norfolk NR25 6HP
www.old-town.co.uk

Thank Yous

Special thanks to Dee Rettali for her enormous contribution to our food offer over the last three years, in particular the sourdough cakes.

Also, to all those who have worked for Fernandez & Wells; in particular Marcelo, for all his hard work and amazing dedication to the cause. Justin Savage for his hand and eye, and Tim Harvey for his generous help and design skills. The numerous others for their support and friendship, including Anita LeRoy for her inspiration, plus Karen Jones, Michael Polemis, Nick Lander and Jack Coleman.

Our suppliers, including especially Elliott and Alison of the Ham & Cheese Company; Jon and Jane at Mons Cheesemongers; Neal's Yard Dairy; Aleem at Seven Seeded Bakery; Julian at Juan Pedro Domecq; Stephen Leighton at Has Bean Coffee; Tim at Postcard Teas; and Paul at TJ Wholesale.

Thanks to Kate Pollard and her team at Hardie Grant for giving us the opportunity to make this book. To Helen Cathcart for the amazing photography and Charlotte Heal for the stunning book design. Also, to our agent, Jonathan Hayden.

Huge thanks to our wives, Cindy and Catherine.

Also the Wells girls: Natalya, Lexi and Ione, who have all done their time in the shops.

And, finally, a big thank you to our loyal customers who have supported us all these years.

About the Authors

Jorge and Rick are the founder-owners of six pioneering cafés in central London, all called Fernandez & Wells, serving simple food and drink from morning until night using timeless quality ingredients.

Jorge is known for his abundant beard and his ceaseless quest for well-crafted kit. Born of Spanish parents, he was brought up in West London, where he met his wife Catherine at school. They have two children, Pablo and Maya, and an English bull terrier called Monty. His working life has revolved around food and drink in one form or another and, in particular, coffee. He owns an old Land Rover and enjoys using it when possible to explore the great outdoors.

Rick is distinguished by his height and inability to walk anywhere slowly. A legacy of early years spent running outdoors in Africa set him in good stead for sporting accolades (chasing balls of various shapes) at school back in England. Further post-university wanderings in Africa led to a career in journalism, mainly with the BBC, where he met his wife Cindy. Her Mediterranean roots and skills in the kitchen complemented his love of wine – attributes passed on to their three daughters, Natalya, Lexi and Ione. He enjoys any opportunity to spend time on a riverbank fly-fishing for brown trout.

Index

RUSTIC by Jorge Fernandez and Rick Wells

First published in 2015 by Hardie Grant Books

Hardie Grant Books (UK)
5th & 6th Floors
52-54 Southwark Street
London SE1 1UN
www.hardiegrant.co.uk

Hardie Grant Books (Australia)
Ground Floor, Building 1
658 Church Street
Melbourne, VIC 3121
www.hardiegrant.com.au

British Library Cataloguing-in-Publication Data. A catalogue record
for this book is available from the British Library.

ISBN: 978-1-78488-011-8

Publisher: Kate Pollard
Senior Editor: Kajal Mistry
Photographer: Helen Cathcart
Photographer's assistant: River Thompson
Recipe writer and food stylist: Dee Rettali
Design and Art Direction: Charlotte Heal Design
Illustrator: Katrin Coetzer
Prop stylist: Linda Berlin
Copy editor: Susan Pegg
Proofreader: Kay Delves
Indexer: Cathy Heath
Colour Reproduction by p2d
Printed and bound in China by 1010

10 9 8 7 6 5 4 3 2 1